ASSESSING ACADEMIC
PROGRAMS IN
HIGHER EDUCATION

ASSESSING ACADEMIC PROGRAMS IN HIGHER EDUCATION

Mary J. Allen

California State University
Institute for Teaching and Learning

ANKER PUBLISHING COMPANY, INC.
Bolton, Massachusetts

Assessing Academic Programs in Higher Education

ISBN 1-882982-67-3

Composition by Beverly Jorgensen/Studio J Graphic Design
Cover design by Frederick Schneider/Grafis

Anker Publishing Company, Inc.
176 Ballville Road
P.O. Box 249
Bolton, MA 01740-0249 USA

www.ankerpub.com

DEDICATION

To my husband, Carey, and my colleague in assessment, faculty
development, and teaching, Richard Noel.

About the Author

Mary J. Allen is director of the California State University Institute for Teaching and Learning and former director of the Faculty Teaching & Learning Center and Assessment Center at California State University, Bakersfield. She earned a master's degree in statistics and a Ph.D. in psychology from the University of California, Berkeley, and she taught these subjects for over two decades before branching into faculty development and assessment. She serves as a thinking partner on educational effectiveness for the Western Association of Schools and Colleges (WASC); is Executive Editor of *Exchanges*, the California State University online journal on teaching and learning; and regularly presents workshops on assessment, including the AAHE/WASC collaborative workshop, Building Learner-Centered Institutions: Developing Institutional Strategies for Assessing & Improving Student Learning.

TABLE OF CONTENTS

PREFACE

In 1997, my campus was preparing for an accreditation visit, and it became clear that we had to make rapid strides in assessment. Moving into assessment requires an initial steep learning curve, and I was lucky to undertake this challenge with some of my favorite colleagues–Richard Noel, Beth Rienzi, and J. Daniel McMillin. With a small budget and a lot of determination, we formed the Program Assessment Consultation Team (PACT), and the four of us began reviewing the assessment literature and planning how we could support our campus. We were pleased to learn that assessment was more than just surveys and tests; and we concluded that assessment, as an integral component of learner-centered teaching, had the potential to profoundly impact courses, curricula, and institutions.

None of us, as individuals, had all the skills required for assessment, but collectively we had backgrounds in program evaluation, statistics, psychometrics, survey research, interviewing, and focus groups. Together we wrote the first PACT Handbook, a collection of advice based on what we were learning and a review of various assessment strategies, and we used it as a workbook for assessment workshops. We shared the Handbook with a few colleagues, and soon began getting requests for copies and more workshops. Richard Noel and I, alone or together, have offered assessment workshops to over 2,000 faculty, administrators, and staff; and as we learned more, the PACT Handbook grew.

The Handbook was not meant to be a stand-alone book. We created it for workshops. But it became clear that much of what happens in those workshops could be integrated with Handbook materials to provide what we did in the workshops–realistic, pragmatic support to busy professionals who want to develop or improve the assessment of their academic programs. I hope this book serves this function. Assessment, for most faculty, requires a major change in how they view course and curriculum design—focusing on the learner, rather than the instructor. Assessment is not rocket science, and it does not have to be the tail that wags the dog. This book should help you develop and implement a meaningful, manageable, and sustainable assessment plan that focuses faculty attention on student learning.

I thank Richard Noel for his many contributions to this book and to my thinking about assessment. Our countless hours of discussion driving to and from assessment workshops, his draft language for several chapters of this book, and his careful feedback on the chapters as they developed have been collegial, insightful, and instrumental. One could not ask for a better colleague, and I wish him a happy retirement!

1

ASSESSING EDUCATIONAL OUTCOMES

Two boys are walking down the street. The first boy says, "I've been really busy this summer. I've been teaching my dog to talk."

His friend responds, "Wow! I can't wait to have a conversation with your dog."

The first boy shakes his head. "I said I've been teaching him. I didn't say he learned anything."

College and university faculty love their disciplines and want to share their knowledge and enthusiasm with students. Unlike the boy in this story, they are not satisfied unless their students are learning. They want their students to learn. Good teachers have always monitored student learning, frequently by unconsciously surveying student faces to find signs of understanding or confusion. Many faculty make this monitoring more systematic by integrating classroom assessment into their courses, allowing them to adjust course activities to improve student attainment (Angelo & Cross, 1993). This approach can be extended to entire programs. While classroom assessment examines learning in the day-to-day classroom, program assessment systematically examines student attainment in the entire curriculum.

A cultural change is occurring in higher education toward increased emphasis on student learning (American Association for Higher Education [AAHE], American College Personnel Association [ACPA], & National Association of Student Personnel Administrators [NASPA], 1998; Weimer, 2002). This learner-centered approach focuses on engaging students in an environment that promotes learning. The emphasis is on what students learn and what students do. Faculty work collaboratively to decide what they want students to learn, and they develop courses and curricula to systematically help students synthesize, practice, and develop increasingly complex ideas, skills, and values. Assessment is an integral component of this approach. Assessment involves the use of empirical data on student learning to refine programs and improve student learning.

Agencies which accredit colleges and universities and their specialized programs are well aware of these trends in higher education, and they have been a major force promoting the use of assessment (Lopez, 1999; Wright, 2002). Although colleges and universities have considerable autonomy, most faculty, students, and others want to be associated with accredited campuses and programs. When accrediting bodies require assessment, campuses pay attention. Assessment, though, should be implemented because it promotes student learning, not because an external agency requires it. This book would not be complete without a discussion of accreditation expectations, and that topic will be addressed later in this chapter.

CHANGES IN HIGHER EDUCATION

The author of this book has been in higher education for over three decades, and the teaching and learning environment has changed in many ways over this period. These changes have led to increased faculty attention to assessing our impact on students. Program assessment is best understood in this context as a best practice in higher education.

Students have become more and more diverse (Baxter Magolda & Terenzini, 2002). Most faculty see increasing variety in many characteristics, such as writing and mathematics skills, English fluency, computer literacy, cultural background, world and work experiences, and learning styles. Faculty are challenged to find ways to engage *all* students in effective learning environments. Traditional teaching methods may not be the most effective for all learners in today's classrooms. Assessment allows us to determine which pedagogical approaches work and for whom.

Educational theorists have developed new conceptions of how students learn and how faculty should promote learning (AAHE, ACPA, & NASPA, 1998; Barr & Tagg, 1995). Earlier teaching models, primarily based on delivering content through textbooks and lecturing, assumed that students learn through listening, reading, and independent work. Typical grading practices, based on grading on a curve, frequently put students into competition with each other, discouraging student collaboration. More recent conceptions of learning stress that students construct knowledge by integrating new learning into what they already know. Learning is viewed as a cognitive and social process in which students construct meaning through reflection and through their interactions with faculty, fellow students, and others. This approach involves expanded use of active learning pedagogies, such as collaborative and cooperative learning, problem-based learning, and community service learning. Our ability to meet the educational needs of our diverse student body depends on developing an expanded repertoire of pedagogical strategies with demonstrated effectiveness, and assessment helps us identify these strategies.

What faculty teach has changed, too (Halpern & Associates, 1994; Weimer, 2002). Knowledge is expanding so rapidly that thorough content coverage is not feasible in most disciplines. Representatives of the Association of American Colleges and Universities (2002) have concluded that "the explosion of readily available information means that being able to find out what one needs to know has begun to replace knowledge itself as an educated person's hallmark" (Our Nation Goes to College Because . . . section, ¶ 1). Faculty must make decisions about what they want students to learn. They have accepted responsibility for helping students become educated adults, and that involves more than mastery of a single discipline. We want our students to be able to integrate what they learn to solve complex problems. Writing-across-the-curriculum initiatives have encouraged faculty to help all students become better writers, and similar initiatives for critical thinking, information competency, interdisciplinary thinking, multicultural understanding, and oral communication have emerged. In addition, faculty are aware that students have to develop the ability and inclination for life-

3

long learning, and they are working to find ways to embed this in the curriculum. New expectations for student learning lead faculty to focus more on process than on content, to consider new ways to assess learning, and to examine the effects of changes in curricular focus.

Technological developments also have affected teaching and learning (Novak, Patterson, Gavrin, & Christian, 1999). Faculty are finding effective ways to use technology in "smart" classrooms and to offer educational opportunities to distant and asynchronous learners. Unlike lectures and books, the Internet allows students to follow links to explore course materials in idiosyncratic ways and to communicate asynchronously with faculty and peers at times that fit their busy schedules. While faculty are experimenting with technology-assisted teaching, some students are experimenting with technology-assisted cheating, such as cyber-plagiarism and the use of electronic communication devices during exams. Faculty and students interact in a rapidly changing technological environment. As faculty integrate technology into their courses and as campuses develop virtual programs, we ask questions about their effectiveness relative to traditional courses and programs. Assessment allows us to answer these questions.

New models of faculty roles have emerged in this context. Faculty less often are the sage on the stage and more often view themselves as designers of learning environments or choreographers of student learning (Honan, 2002). Faculty have recognized the need to evaluate the impact of their teaching on learning among all their students, and over 150 journals publish scholarship of teaching research in a wide variety of disciplines (Scholarship of Teaching & Learning at Indiana University Bloomington, 2002). Assessment engages faculty in reflection on what they and their students are accomplishing, and this is an important component of their professional roles. "Assessment is part and parcel of the teaching/learning process" (Association of American Colleges and Universities, 2002, We Can Ensure Ongoing Improvement by . . . section, ¶ 3).

WHAT IS PROGRAM ASSESSMENT?

As a whole, assessment is a framework for focusing faculty attention on student learning and for provoking meaningful discussions of program objectives, curricular organization, pedagogy, and student development.

Such discussions should be normal components of faculty life; however, many faculty report that responding to assessment demands led to the first formal, department-wide discussion of curriculum and instruction in decades. This is an important, immediate benefit of engaging in program assessment.

Program assessment is an ongoing process designed to monitor and improve student learning. Faculty develop explicit statements of what students should learn, verify that the program is designed to foster this learning, collect empirical data that indicate student attainment, and use these data to improve student learning. Conversations about what faculty expect their students to learn almost invariably lead to a discussion of the alignment of pedagogy and curriculum with these expectations, and this analysis can lead to curricular improvements *before* traditional outcomes data are collected. Chapter 3 expands on this concept of alignment.

Learning objectives are statements of what students are expected to learn. For example, objectives for an undergraduate psychology major might include statements that graduates can:

1) Write research reports in APA style.

2) Apply APA guidelines for the ethical treatment of human research participants to research plans.

3) Communicate effectively and sensitively with people from diverse cultural backgrounds.

These objectives should be consistent with campus and program missions. For example, faculty who teach in programs with a human services focus might have different objectives, such as graduates can:

1) Write clinical reports that meet agency needs.

2) Integrate ethical guidelines for clinical practice into their work with clients.

3) Provide services effectively and sensitively to people from diverse cultural backgrounds.

Curricula should be aligned with learning objectives because students cannot be expected to master objectives if they aren't given appropriate learning opportunities. For example, students are unlikely to develop strong information competence skills if they are never provided appropriate instruction, assignments, and feedback.

It is important to recognize that faculty do not have to collect information from every student every year on every objective! Many faculty are accustomed to collecting research data from samples, and the same strategy can be applied to collecting assessment data. Programs generally are subject to periodic review cycles, with formal program review every five to seven years. Faculty can develop an assessment plan that systematically examines learning objectives across this period, and they can give priority to objectives that they value most highly. In this way, assessment results in incremental improvements in curriculum and pedagogy. Notice that this model involves ongoing assessment. Rather than focusing on evaluating the program every five or seven years, faculty are engaged in assessment every year. Assessment is as much a part of their role as grading and holding office hours. You can judge how far your assessment program has progressed by comparing it to the stages described in Figure 1.1. Even on the same campus, departments and individuals within departments often vary in their commitment to assessment, but at its best, assessment is viewed as an indispensable tool for focusing faculty attention on student learning.

The bottom line for assessment is student learning. Assessment should be done because faculty are professional educators who want to ensure that the learning environments they provide support the development of their students.

KEY ASSESSMENT VOCABULARY

The glossary at the end of this book summarizes some key assessment terms. Standardized assessment vocabulary has not been firmly established, so when you read about assessment, be aware that terms might be used in different ways.

Assessments can provide *direct* or *indirect* measures of student learning. Direct measures require students to demonstrate their achievement. For example, say you were teaching students to juggle. Perhaps you

---

Figure 1.1
Steps in a Campus Assessment Program

Denial: It's a fad. If I ignore it, it will go away.

Acceptance: OK, I guess we have to do it.

Resistance: I feel threatened. My department feels threatened. My campus feels threatened. Can I subvert it by not participating in the process or in some other way?

Understanding: Maybe we can learn something useful. Can we use what we've already been doing?

Campaign: We have a plan. Maybe it's not perfect, but let's get moving!

Collaboration: We have a plan with long-range objectives that are clearly defined, and, based on our experience with assessment, we believe it works.

Institutionalization: We can't imagine working without assessment. It's a permanent part of our institutional culture.

Adapted from Wehlburg (1999).

---

would be satisfied with student progress if 90% of your students could juggle three tennis balls in a two-foot arc for five minutes. Indirect assessment is based on opinions. You could ask graduates of your juggling class to indicate if their juggling skills have improved, perhaps using a rating scale that runs from "0" (no improvement) to "4" (substantial improvement). You might be satisfied if no students gave a rating of 0 and at least 80% of the ratings are 2 or higher. You could obtain the opinions of others, too. For example, you might invite a professional juggler to rate the quality of students' juggling. If standards are met, you are satisfied. If not, then you must decide how to address this deficiency.

Another distinction is between *traditional* and *performance* measurement. Traditional measurements are based on the types of tests most of us took when we were in college, such as multiple-choice and true-false exams. Performance measurements, such as the above juggling test, require students to directly demonstrate their learning. Piano recitals by music students are performance tests, but an essay test asking students to describe aspects of piano playing would be traditional measurement. Similarly, you could directly assess information competence by following students to the library and observing how well they locate relevant sources (performance measurement), or you could ask them traditional exam questions about relevant search engines. High scores on traditional tests are assumed to indicate mastery, but most of us know students whose academic skills are stronger than their practical skills when faced with actual clients or complex problems. This is why most experts suggest that we use multiple measures of our objectives. If different types of measures *triangulate* (i.e., lead to the same conclusion), we have more confidence in the accuracy of conclusions.

Another commonly used phrase is *authentic assessment.* Authentic assessment involves real-world activities that professionals in the discipline encounter. For example, accounting students could be asked to audit a set of actual or simulated accounting records and social work students could be asked to make recommendations about real or simulated clients. Authentic assessments also can be conducted at fieldwork sites in which students work with clients or address problems. Fieldwork supervisors could be enlisted to assess student mastery of learning objectives, perhaps using rating scales or rubrics that provide criteria for making judgments.

Assessments can result in *quantitative* or *qualitative* data. Quantitative data involve numerical scores that indicate how much students have learned. Scores are based on exams, papers, projects, or other evidence of student learning, and they frequently are summarized using descriptive statistics, such as the mean, standard deviation, and range. Qualitative data do not involve numerical scores and are described verbally. They may be based on interviews, focus groups, or responses to open-ended survey questions. The qualitative analysis involves writing a useful description of what was learned.

Assessments can involve *value-added* or *absolute* judgments. The distinction is whether the assessment is of change or of absolute performance. For example, faculty who teach a recreational swimming course might phrase their learning objective in value-added terms: Students who complete the course will improve their swimming ability. They might be satisfied if one student moves from being afraid of the water to swimming one lap and another student improves from swimming one lap to swimming several laps. Alternatively, these faculty might have absolute expectations: Students who complete the course will be able to swim at least four consecutive laps. These faculty will be satisfied only if students meet this expectation. Value-added assessment generally involves comparing two measurements that establish baseline and final performance, but sometimes baseline data are not available and value-added criteria are assessed by comparing groups, such as sophomores and seniors.

Sometimes assessment data are collected under special circumstances, such as Assessment Days in which classes are cancelled and students are invited to participate in campus assessment programs. Alternatively, assessment activities can be *embedded* within courses. For example, all faculty who teach a research methods course may agree to embed a question on research ethics in their final exams. Student responses to this question are used to grade them within their courses, and these same responses are analyzed to assess student mastery of relevant objectives. Students are likely to be motivated to demonstrate the extent of their learning on embedded assessments because they also are being graded on their performance, but they may not work as hard on Assessment Day tests if they view results as not having any personal consequences.

Assessment data can serve *formative* or *summative* purposes. Formative assessment provides feedback to improve what is being assessed, and summative assessment provides an evaluative summary. For example, a student paper receives a C+ (summative assessment), and comments are written in the margins to help the student improve (formative assessment). External reviewers may do program assessments with an emphasis on formative or summative goals. For example, they may be charged to do a summative evaluation of the quality of the curriculum, or they may be invited to do a formative assessment and provide recommendations for its improvement. Program assessment, as treated in this book, is for formative purposes—to improve the quality of student learning.

Developmental assessment tracks the development of individual students, and data can be summarized for all students to assess the program. Programs that use developmental assessment may have a series of checkpoints or hurdles ("progression exams"), and students may be required to meet specific standards before they can continue. For example, students

9

may be required to pass "riser exams" before they are allowed into upper-division coursework. The proportion of students who pass sections of the riser exam could be used to assess the overall effectiveness of the lower-division program for helping students master the relevant learning objectives. Sometimes students are given "prescriptions" for additional work if their performance does not meet expectations. For example, students may be required to repeat an ethics course before beginning fieldwork if the developmental assessment indicates insufficient understanding of relevant ethical principles. Developmental assessment may be particularly relevant in professional programs, such as teacher education, because degree completion may certify graduates for immediate entry into careers.

ASSESSMENT STEPS

Six basic steps underlie the assessment of student learning:

1) Develop learning objectives.

2) Check for alignment between the curriculum and the objectives.

3) Develop an assessment plan.

4) Collect assessment data.

5) Use results to improve the program.

6) Routinely examine the assessment process and correct, as needed.

As described above, the first steps are to develop learning objectives and to check for the alignment between the curriculum and objectives. Chapter 2 focuses on how faculty can develop statements of their learning objectives, and Chapter 3 describes aligning curricula with objectives.

Once faculty are assured that students receive opportunities to master objectives, they should develop an assessment plan. The plan describes how faculty will systematically assess the learning objectives and answers the big questions: who, what, when, where, how? This plan should describe a process that will generate meaningful data and that will be manageable and sustainable. Assessment is important, but it is not all that faculty do. It is better to develop a realistic plan that takes foreseeable constraints into account than to try to do too much, because attempting too much is likely to result in the trivialization or abandonment of assessment efforts (Maki, 2002c; Nichols, 1995). Chapter 4 describes assessment planning.

The next step is to implement the assessment plan by collecting and analyzing assessment data. Chapters 5 through 7 describe a variety of strategies for doing this. It is important that faculty identify techniques they are comfortable with, so they will be interested in results and willing to act on them.

Step 5 probably is the hardest. Faculty and campuses are wonderful data collectors, as most of us know, but data which are filed away without analysis are useless. As they say in the Midwest, "You can't fatten a pig by weighing it." Results should be used to improve the program. The phrase used most often in this context is "close the loop." Faculty discuss assessment results and reach conclusions about what results mean. They identify which learning objectives have been mastered at acceptable levels and which learning objectives require more attention. They determine implications for changes in curriculum or pedagogy, and they decide how to implement modifications. Good assessment leads to collective reflection and action.

The last step is sometimes forgotten. Faculty should think of each assessment study as a pilot project and examine the study itself. The assessment plan should not be set in concrete. If faculty find flaws in an assessment plan, they should change it. Repeatedly collecting problematic data is an exercise in futility, and faculty have better things to do with their time. Chapter 8 provides more information on effective assessment efforts.

DIFFERENCES BETWEEN GRADING AND ASSESSMENT

At this point you might be asking a pressing question: Why should faculty do all this work to assess student learning when they already routinely examine student attainment to assign grades? Don't students' transcripts indicate how well students have learned?

Grades do indicate something about student learning, but at a level too broad for meaningful assessment. If the average GPA of program graduates is 2.89, which learning objectives are being mastered and which require faculty attention? Similarly, if the average grade for students in a course is 2.75, which learning objectives associated with this course have been mastered?

Other differences between grading and assessment exist. An important aspect of grading is to create transcripts that have *summative validity*; that is, transcripts accurately summarize overall student attainment. Transcripts are high stakes for students because they are used to certify graduation requirements, and they influence entry into careers, graduate programs, and other opportunities. Assessment, though, is a formative process, and formative validity is more important than summative validity—it is more important that assessment projects result in meaningful improvements to curricula and pedagogy than that they provide precise summaries of the achievement of individual students. Qualitative techniques are sometimes avoided when grading students because they are perceived as being too subjective, but such techniques have an important place in assessment, especially when these subjective judgments are respected by faculty who plan and offer the curriculum.

Grading focuses on individuals, and individual students are associated with their grades. When we grade, measurement precision is important so each grade reflects individual attainment. When we assign a B+ to one student and a B to another, we are claiming that we made an equitable distinction between these students and that the first student's course performance was better than the second's. In addition, course grades are generated based on student success in individual courses. Exams and assignments may focus on course-specific content, rather than on broader learning objectives, and course grades may reflect relatively short-term learning—knowledge that is forgotten after the final exam is completed.

The emphasis on measurement precision becomes less important in assessment because individual students are not identified. Generally, anonymity, confidentiality, and privacy are preserved. Assessment studies are used to inform conclusions about student mastery of learning objectives. Data are aggregated across students, and measurement errors due to measurement imprecision cancel out unless there is a systematic bias to overestimate or underestimate achievement. Assessment data should not be sloppy or deliberately imprecise, but measurement precision is less important when collecting assessment data than when collecting data to grade students. This, again, is why subjective judgments often play a larger role in assessment than in assigning grades. Program assessment focuses on broad learning objectives that cut across courses in the curriculum, placing more emphasis on the integration of learning and long-term retention, so it may require different types of data than typical course grading.

WHY SHOULD FACULTY DO ASSESSMENT?

Faculty are busy people. They serve increasingly diverse student populations, they experiment with new pedagogies, they maintain currency with technological changes, and their personal and professional lives make conflicting demands on their time. Why should they take on one more responsibility: program assessment?

Teaching and learning at colleges and universities are components of a complex process. Faculty can improve the quality of this process through engaging in assessment. Assessment data allow them to confirm assumptions about student progress and to identify discrepancies about what students actually learn. They can use assessment results to make informed decisions about pedagogical or curricular changes, and they can use assessment data as baseline information for demonstrating the impact of curricular innovations. Assessment should lead to improved student mastery of learning objectives that faculty value, an ample reward for faculty who take teaching and learning seriously. In addition, as Maki (2002b) points out, intellectual curiosity is the basis for much of what faculty do. Faculty should be curious to learn how their teaching impacts student learning and, as rational decision-makers, they should want to reflect on evidence, rather than rely on conjecture, to guide decision-making. Facione and Facione (1996) agree:

> Bright people have real anxieties with regard to why they are being asked to engage in student outcomes assessment. The culture of the faculty on most campuses would find the call to student outcomes assessment threatening, insulting, intrusive, and wrongheaded. But, in the final analysis, committed faculty want their students to learn. (¶ 8)

Assessment should not be the tail that wags the dog. Embedding assessment within what faculty and students normally do, such as targeting program learning objectives in course assignments and exams, allows faculty to conduct meaningful assessment studies without adding excessive amounts of extra work to their lives. Even in departments without formal assessment programs, faculty often are aware of gaps in student mastery of program objectives, but these notions are often anecdotal in nature and not systematically addressed. Assessment focuses faculty attention on the use of evidence to guide planning.

America's professoriate is graying, and many new faculty will be hired in the next decade. In addition, many departments make extensive use of part-time or temporary faculty. Having statements of program objectives and clear understanding of how the curriculum aligns with these objectives allows departments to clarify program needs when recruiting faculty and to communicate expectations to them. Too often in the past, new faculty were shown a catalog description and turned loose to generate their courses, with little attention to how these courses contributed to a cohesive curriculum.

Involvement in assessment can be useful to individual faculty. Assessment should give them a better overview of the curriculum and how their teaching activities contribute to student learning. In addition, they may become better able to contribute to the growing literature on the scholarship of teaching or to identify grant opportunities based on their ability to define, measure, and help students master meaningful objectives.

Assessment can lead to better communication with others about what we are doing. Programs can use assessment information for public relations–communicating success stories to funding bodies, administrators, and prospective students and their families. Accrediting agencies require faculty engagement in assessment programs and the use of assessment results to improve student learning. Some states require or are considering performance-based funding based on the assessment of outcomes. Campuses that fail to take the lead in this effort run the risk of having people less informed about their mission and institution impose ill-conceived or inappropriate assessment processes and criteria.

Competition in higher education is increasing. Students can select among alternative institutions, including national and international college systems and Internet-based universities. Nontraditional providers tend to have highly articulated objectives and supportive assessment data (e.g., Klor De Alva & Slobodzian, 2001; Scarafiotti, 2001). Faculty may need to demonstrate the uniqueness and quality of learning in their programs to maintain program viability.

CAMPUS POLITICS AND POLICIES

Every campus has its own culture, and this culture may prevent or promote meaningful assessment. The engagement of program faculty in the process is essential (AAHE, 2002; Association of American Colleges and Universities, 2002; Middle States Commission on Higher Education, 1996), and campus policies should reward and encourage their participation.

Collegiality among program faculty is essential. Agreeing on learning objectives, checking for program alignment, developing an assessment plan, collecting data, using results, and examining assessment practices are not tasks for one person; they especially are not tasks for an outsider who is not aware of your program mission or student needs. Assessment is not something that someone does *to* you or *for* you; it is the responsibility of the faculty who control and offer the program. The assessment process is more likely to have a positive impact on program functioning if faculty collectively agree upon what is important, buy into assessment strategies, and are flexible to correct identified problems. This is the goal, and campus policies should promote faculty collegiality and involvement.

Faculty report that trust is essential–they must be able to trust that their peers will not unfairly retaliate for differences of opinion or unexpected results. Occasionally new, untenured faculty members are given assessment responsibilities, and they sometimes express legitimate fears that senior faculty will "shoot the messenger" if results do not support their preconceptions. Faculty also need to trust administrators and others who will learn about assessment results. They are concerned that deans or provosts might punish departments that assess difficult-to-reach objectives and reward departments that assess easy-to-reach objectives. Policies and practices must reward faculty and programs that are willing to examine important, challenging learning objectives.

Faculty also are concerned that personnel decisions might be affected by assessment results. Campus policies should reward faculty who take leadership roles in program assessment because it is an important task that takes time away from other activities. Faculty should be allowed to use relevant assessment information in their personnel files, as long as the privacy and confidentiality of colleagues are protected. However, requirements that program assessment data be analyzed separately for individual faculty are not recommended. At the 1999 annual meeting of the Higher Learning Commission, Lopez (1999) concludes that "The mantra on every campus must be: 'assessment is about student learning; it is not about faculty evaluation'" (p. 13). Assessment data should be aggregated across faculty and courses because they should be used to assess the entire program. If personnel decisions are based on assessment data, faculty may seek ways to undermine the process. They may choose not to participate in assessment activities that threaten their integrity or careers, or they may trivialize the process rather than endanger themselves or their program.

Campus and program faculty should articulate policies about the use of assessment data. Who has access to program data? What level of detail leaves faculty hands? Program faculty, of course, require access to assessment details, but raw data from assessment projects might be summarized first, with identifying information for students and faculty removed. For example, when focus groups are used for program assessment, summaries should not identify individual faculty by name. The goal of assessment is to assess student learning in the program, not to identify scapegoats or provide details for personnel decisions. Administrators should have reasonable access to assessment findings, but they probably do not need the same level of detail as program faculty. Some campuses require departments to file annual assessment reports that summarize what was done, what was learned, and what impact the assessment had on program functioning. This allows administrators to monitor campus assessment activities, to identify programs that require extra encouragement or assistance, and to identify programs with assessment expertise that might be shared with others. Administrators and relevant campus governing bodies should expect the use of relevant assessment evidence to support budget and curricular requests. Assessment findings should guide decision-making.

Faculty are rarely exposed to outcomes assessment techniques in their graduate training, and the assessment literature is growing rapidly.

In addition, not all faculty have expertise in empirical research, so some will need additional assistance to move into assessment. Campuses should establish appropriate training opportunities and support services. Some campuses have professionally staffed assessment centers; others award time to a person or team to develop and share expertise. Campuses may bring in consultants, send faculty to assessment conferences, provide internal assessment grants, publish assessment newsletters, and host assessment forums for faculty to learn from each other. Faculty in some programs may need local support for the development of learning objectives and the selection and implementation of assessment procedures, including assistance in data analysis. Some assessment procedures, such as interviews and focus groups, often work best when conducted by impartial outsiders, and campuses should find ways to support such activities. Assessment takes time and support. It does not come for free, and administrators may have to provide start-up funds or incentives for programs to move forward, as well as support for ongoing assessment activities.

Closing the loop (using results to make curricular or pedagogical changes) may be especially difficult if faculty do not have the flexibility to make curricular changes or are not aware of alternative teaching methods. Campus curricular policies should respect well-informed faculty decisions to effect changes. Faculty development opportunities that engage faculty in reflection on their teaching and that provide information and assistance on new pedagogies may be essential for effective change.

Teachers and students do not interact in a vacuum. Students who cannot buy textbooks because their financial aid checks are delayed, who lack access to materials when they participate in online courses, or who need counseling or tutoring assistance that is only available during their work hours will not be able to fully benefit from their coursework. Although this book emphasizes program assessment focusing on student mastery of learning objectives, effective change may require the coordinated effort of faculty and other campus professionals who support students. Many campuses create formal structures to promote the types of communication and problem solving required for campus professionals to assess and improve what they do. As a joint committee of the American Association for Higher Education, the American College Personnel

Association, and the National Association of Student Personnel Administrators (1998) concluded,

> Despite American higher education's success at providing collegiate education for an unprecedented number of people, the vision of equipping all our students with learning deep enough to meet the challenges of the post-industrial age provides us with a powerful incentive to do our work better. . . . only when everyone on campus–particularly academic affairs and student affairs staff–shares the responsibility for student learning will we be able to make significant progress in improving it. (¶ 1)

Assessment provides a context for important discussions of how to work together to accomplish this goal.

ACCREDITATION

Accrediting organizations certify that institutions and programs have appropriate infrastructure, policies, and services to support their operations and that they are accomplishing their missions. They generally focus on two major issues: capacity and effectiveness. Capacity involves questions about financial stability, physical plant (classrooms, offices, computers, libraries, etc.), governance structure, faculty, policies, catalogs, enrollment histories, and student support services. In addition, institutions are expected to operate with integrity in their relationships with accreditors, funders, other institutions, employees, and students. Accreditors must certify that institutions or programs have the capacity to execute their mission; and the mission may be one of a major research university, a regional comprehensive university, a small liberal arts college, a specialized campus (such as a dental college), or a professional program housed within a larger institution.

Accrediting organizations require serious examination of educational effectiveness, and they expect campuses to document their impact on student learning. Accreditors certify that campuses and programs have quality assurance mechanisms in place, and program assessment provides the context for monitoring and improving the quality of academic programs. Just as the bottom line in business is the generation of profit, the bottom line in higher education is the generation of learning. Although institutions may have excellent capacity, as indicated by outstanding library holdings, faculty with exceptional academic credentials, and labs equipped with the latest technology, they are still expected to demonstrate that their students have learned.

Six major regional accrediting organizations serve geographical segments of the United States (see Appendix 1.1). They accredit entire institutions, rather than single programs within them, and they expect programs within these institutions to have active assessment programs that impact program functioning. *Impact* is the key word here. Assessment requires more than just collecting data; assessment involves using results to effect change. Sample statements from regional accreditation standards are provided in Appendix 1.2.

Institutions that serve a national or international student body may be accredited by one or more agencies. For example, The University of Phoenix Online is accredited by the North Central Association. Sometimes accrediting bodies work together. For example, an Interregional Accrediting Committee (IRAC) was created by North Central, Northwestern, and Western regional accreditors to oversee the accreditation program for the Western Governors University.

In addition to the regional commissions, other national accrediting bodies are associated with the Council for Higher Education Accreditation (CHEA), and many professional programs have program-specific accrediting organizations associated with the Association of Specialized and Professional Accreditors (ASPA). These specialized accreditors review individual programs within universities as well as entire colleges or universities that offer specialized programs, such as medical schools, and they often provide lists of required learning objectives. You may have noticed a lot of "alphabet soup" in this section, and more is to come. Faculty in relevant disciplines know these accreditors by their acronyms, and these are provided here. Appendix 1.3 lists these specialized accrediting bodies.

Accrediting organizations are subject to review by the Council for Higher Education Accreditation, which has the ultimate authority to *recognize* American accreditation agencies. CHEA (1998) explicitly requires that "accrediting organizations have standards that encourage institutions to plan, where needed, for purposeful change and improvement; to develop and sustain activities that anticipate and address needed change; to stress student achievement; and to ensure long-range institutional viability" (p. 2). Accreditation should involve "faculty and staff comprehensively in institutional evaluation and planning" (Office of Postsecondary Education, 2002, Some Functions of Accreditation section), and program assessment is an essential component of this process. Most accrediting bodies expect to see ongoing program assessment and the use of assessment data for decision-making, and program faculty should expect to demonstrate the extent and impact of their assessment activities during self studies and accreditation visits. Assessment is more than a fad. It is an integral part of higher education.

Although accrediting organizations have provided major motivation to many institutions, meaningful, sustainable assessment of academic programs will not emerge unless faculty integrate assessment into their normal work. Research suggests that campuses that primarily do assessment to comply with accreditation requirements are less likely to have assessment programs that impact campus functioning (National Center for Postsecondary Improvement, 2002). As Maki (2002b) noted, "Viewed as externally mandated, assessment of student learning typically ebbs and flows within an institution in relation to the timing of accreditation visits" (¶ 1). Assessment, properly executed, is an ongoing activity, not one that emerges every ten years, and it is an intrinsic component of effective student development. As Tom Angelo (1999), former director of the American Association for Higher Education Assessment Forum, reminds us, "Though accountability matters, learning still matters most" (¶ 1).

Appendix 1.1
List of Regional Accrediting Bodies

Organization	Primary Region	Web Site
Middle States Association of Colleges and Schools (MSA)	Delaware, the District of Columbia, Maryland, New Jersey, New York, Pennsylvania, Puerto Rico, the US Virgin Islands, the Republic of Panama	http://www.msache.org/
New England Association of Schools and Colleges (NEASC)	Connecticut, Maine, Massachusetts, New Hampshire, Rhode Island, Vermont	http://www.neasc.org/
North Central Association of Colleges and Schools (NCS)	Arizona, Arkansas, Colorado, Illinois, Indiana, Iowa, Kansas, Michigan, Minnesota, Missouri, Nebraska, New Mexico, North Dakota, Ohio, Oklahoma, South Dakota, West Virginia, Wisconsin, Wyoming, including schools of the Navajo Nation	http://www.nca/higherlearningcommission.org/
Northwest Association of Schools and of Colleges and Universities	Alaska, Idaho, Montana, Nevada, Oregon, Utah, Washington	http://www.nwccu.org/
Southern Association of Colleges and Schools (SACS)	Alabama, Florida, Georgia, Kentucky, Louisiana, Mississippi, North Carolina, South Carolina, Tennessee, Texas, Virginia	http://www.sacs.org/
Western Association of Schools and Colleges (WASC)	California, Hawaii, the US territories of Guam and American Samoa, the Republic of Palau, the Federated States of Micronesia, the Commonwealth of the Northern Marianna Islands, the Republic of the Marshall Islands	http://www.wascweb.org/

APPENDIX 1.2
SAMPLE ACCREDITATION STATEMENTS CONCERNING PROGRAM ASSESSMENT

Regional Accreditation Body	Statements
Middle States	"Assessment of student learning demonstrates that the institution's students have knowledge, skills, and competencies consistent with institutional goals and that students at graduation have achieved appropriate higher education goals. . . . In order to carry out meaningful assessment activities, institutions must articulate statements of expected student learning at the institutional, program, and individual course levels. . . . Course syllabi or guidelines should include expected learning outcomes. . . . Assessment is not an event but a process and should be an integral part of the life of the institution. . . . Finally, and most significantly, a commitment to assessment of student learning requires a parallel commitment to ensuring its use." (*Characteristics of Excellence in Higher Education: Eligibility Requirements and Standards for Accreditation.* [2002]. Standard 14: Assessment of Student Learning, pp. 50-51. Available: www.msache.org/pubs.html)
North Central	"The Commission appreciates that effective assessment can take a variety of forms and involve a variety of processes. However, faculty members, with meaningful input from students and strong support from the administration and governing board, should have the fundamental role in developing and sustaining systematic assessment of student learning. Their assessment strategy should be informed by the organization's mission and include explicit public statements regarding the knowledge, skills, and competencies students should possess as a result of completing course and program requirements; it also should document the values, attitudes, and behaviors faculty expect students to have developed. . . . More than just an effective strategy for accountability or an effective management process for curriculum improvement, assessment of student achievement is essential for each higher learning organization that values its effect on the learning of its students." (*Commission Statement on Assessment of Student Learning.* [2003, February 21], ¶ 3. Available: http://www.ncahigherlearningcommission.org/resources/positionstatements/assessment/)

Regional Accreditation Body	Statements
Northwest	• "The institution identifies and publishes the expected learning outcomes for each of its degree and certificate programs. Through regular and systematic assessment, it demonstrates that students who complete their programs, no matter where or how they are offered, have achieved these outcomes." (*Accreditation Handbook.* [1999]. Standard Two-Educational Program and Its Effectiveness. Standard 2.B.2, p. 29. Available: http://www.nwccu.org/Forms/Downloads%20Page.htm) • "The institution provides evidence that its assessment activities lead to the improvement of teaching and learning." (*Accreditation Handbook.* [1999]. Standard Two-Educational Program and Its Effectiveness. Standard 2.B.3, p. 29. Available: http://www.nwccu.org/Forms/Downloads%20Page.htm)
Southern	• "The institution engages in ongoing, integrated, and institution-wide research-based planning and evaluation processes that incorporate a systematic review of programs and services that (a) results in continuing improvement and (b) demonstrates that the institution is accomplishing its mission." (*Principles of Accreditation.* Core Requirements, p. 8. Available: www.sacscoc.org/accrrevproj.asp) • "The institution identifies expected outcomes for its educational programs and its administrative and educational support services; assesses whether it achieves these outcomes; and provides evidence of improvement based on analysis of those results." (*Principles of Accreditation.* Comprehensive Standards, p. 11. Available: www.sacscoc.org/accrrevproj.asp) • "The institution identifies competencies within the general education core and provides evidence that graduates have attained those college-level competencies." (*Principles of Accreditation.* Comprehensive Standards, p. 12. Available: www.sacscoc.org/accrrevproj.asp)

Regional Accreditation Body	Statements
Western	• "All degrees–undergraduate and graduate–awarded by the institution are clearly defined in terms of entry-level requirements and in terms of levels of student achievement necessary for graduation that represent more than simply an accumulation of courses or credits." (*Handbook of Accreditation.* [2001]. Criterion 2.2, p. 20. Available: www.wascweb.org/senior/inst_resource.htm) • "The institution's expectations for learning and student attainment are developed and widely shared among its members (including faculty, students, staff, and where appropriate, external stakeholders). The institution's faculty takes collective responsibility for establishing, reviewing, fostering, and demonstrating the attainment of these expectations." (*Handbook of Accreditation.* [2001]. Criterion 2.3, p. 21. Available: www.wascweb.org/senior/inst_resource.htm) • "The institution demonstrates that its graduates consistently achieve its stated levels of attainment and ensures that its expectations for student learning are embedded in the standards faculty use to evaluate student work." (*Handbook of Accreditation.* [2001]. Criterion 2.6, p. 21. Available: www.wascweb.org/senior/inst_resource.htm) • "In order to improve program currency and effectiveness, all programs offered by the institution are subject to review, including analyses of the achievement of the program's learning objectives and outcomes." (*Handbook of Accreditation.* [2001]. Criterion 2.7, p. 21. Available: www.wascweb.org/senior/inst_resource.htm)

Appendix 1.3
Specialized Accrediting Bodies*

Area	Acronym
Acupuncture*	ACAOM
Advanced Rabbinical and Talmudic Schools**	AARTS
Allied Health*	CAAHEP
Architecture*	NAAB
Art and Design*	NASAD
Bible Colleges**	AABC
Business*	AACSB
Chiropractic*	CCE-CoA
Christian Colleges and Schools**	TRACS
Clinical Laboratory Sciences*	NAACLS
Construction*	ACCE
Counseling*	CACREP
Dance*	NASD
Dentistry*	CDA-ADA
Distance Education and Training**	DETC
Family & Consumer Sciences*	AAFCS-CFA
Forestry*	SAF-CoA
Health Education*	ABHES
Health Services Administration*	ACEHSA
Independent Colleges and Schools**	ACICS
Industrial Technology*	NAIT
Interior Design*	FIDER
Landscape Architecture*	LAAB
Library & Information Studies*	ALA-CoA
Marriage & Family Therapy*	COAMFTE
Medical Education*	LCME
Music*	NASM
Naturopathic Medicine*	CNME

Area	Acronym
Nurse Anesthesia*	COA-NA
Nursing*	CCNE/NLNAC
Occupational Therapy*	ACOTE
Optometry*	ACOE-AOA
Osteopathic Medicine*	AOA
Pharmacy*	ACPE
Physical Therapy*	CAPTE
Physician Assistant*	ARC-PA
Podiatric Medicine*	CPME
Psychoanalysis*	ABAP
Psychology*	APA-CoA
Public Affairs and Administration*	NASPAA-COPRA
Public Health*	CEPH
Rabbinical & Talmudic Education*	AARTS
Radiologic Technology*	JRCERT
Recreation & Parks*	NRPA/AALR-CoA
Rehabilitation Counseling*	CORE
Social Work Education*	CSWE
Speech-Language-Hearing*	ASHA/CAA
Teacher Education*	NCATE
Teacher Education*	TEAC
Teacher Education: Montessori*	MACTE
Theatre*	NAST
Theological Schools**	ATS
Veterinary Medicine*	AVMA-CoE

*See the ASPA web site for contact information: http://www.aspa-usa.org/
**See the CHEA web site for contact information:
http://www.chea.org/Directories/national.cfm

2

DEFINING LEARNING OBJECTIVES

T he first step in program assessment is to determine the program's learning objectives. These objectives guide the development and review of the curriculum and help faculty plan and implement program assessment. Feeling pressured to begin assessment, faculty sometimes try to skip this important step, but this rarely leads to meaningful assessment or program improvement. Faculty also might be tempted to create a set of poorly defined objectives just to quickly satisfy an external mandate. When this occurs, the program and its assessment are trivialized. Faculty owe it to themselves and to their students to develop consensus on the learning objectives that students in their program should master.

Program learning objectives focus attention on the learner. Faculty who are accustomed to traditional, teacher-centered approaches generally focus on what they cover in courses. For example, someone who teaches a course in developmental psychology might cover changes in cognition, personality, and motor skills from birth to early adulthood. The learner-centered approach examines courses and curricula from the other direction. Faculty who teach a developmental psychology course might expect students who complete it to be able to describe changes in cognition, personality, and motor skills from birth to early adulthood; use developmental theories to explain these changes; recognize when children's development requires intervention; and apply what they learn to parenting, education, and public policy issues related to children and families. Although this book emphasizes program objectives, excellent resources are available for the development of course objectives (e.g., Diamond, 1997; Mager, 1997).

Thinking of a course in terms of learning, rather than teaching, can lead to major changes in its structure. Faculty often increase their use of active learning techniques to help students practice the desired skills, and their assignments and grading procedures often are restructured to place greater emphasis on the application of what is learned. Similarly, the development of program learning objectives can lead to changes in the structure of the curriculum, and these changes often involve new expectations for faculty, student, and staff roles. Chapter 3 explores the process of aligning the curriculum with program learning objectives.

Learning objectives focus on knowledge, skills, and values. What should students know? What should they be able to do? What should they value? The objectives are *behavioral*. They describe how students can demonstrate that they have achieved program goals. Some learning objectives were suggested for a developmental psychology course in an earlier paragraph, and these used active verbs–verbs that delineate behaviors (e.g., *describe, use, explain, recognize, apply*). They describe the student behaviors that demonstrate their learning.

Learning objectives should be widely distributed–in the catalog, on the web, in department newsletters, and on syllabi. All major stakeholders, including regular and adjunct faculty, fieldwork supervisors, student support personnel, and students, should be aware of them and should use them to guide course and curriculum planning and learning. Articulating objectives encourages students to be intentional learners who direct and monitor their own learning and encourages faculty to be intentional teachers who cooperate with program colleagues and campus staff to offer a cohesive learning experience. Finally, learning objectives focus assessment efforts and faculty and staff conversations on student learning. They are an essential component of learning-centered teaching.

MISSION, GOALS, AND OBJECTIVES

Faculty should articulate the mission, goals, and learning objectives for their program. The mission is a holistic vision of the values and philosophy of the department, and program goals and objectives describe what faculty want their students to learn.

Every campus has a mission statement, and generally it is provided in the catalog and other campus publications. Each program also should have a mission statement. It communicates a broad vision of the fundamental purposes and values of the program, providing an important view of what matters most to faculty. Effective program mission statements should be consistent with the campus mission statement and should be written in language that can be understood by potential students and their families. The mission statement might provide a brief history of the program and might describe the philosophy of the program; the types of students it serves; the type of professional training it provides; the relative emphasis on teaching, scholarship, and service; and important characteristics of program graduates. For example, the University of Minnesota's College of Agriculture defined this mission: "The mission of the College of Agriculture is to provide students with the educational experiences and environment that promote discipline competence; the capacity to attain career success in agriculture, food, or related professions; and a sense of civic responsibility" (Diamond, 1997, p. 72). This statement guides decision-making about the program.

Program goals are broad statements concerning knowledge, skills, or values that faculty expect graduating students to achieve. They describe general expectations for students, and they should be consistent with the program mission. For example, program goals might state:

- Students know basic biological principles and concepts. (Knowledge)
- Students understand the major theoretical approaches for explaining economic phenomena. (Knowledge)
- Students can use statistical packages to analyze sociological data and can interpret results accurately. (Skill)
- Students have effective interpersonal and leadership skills for entry-level management positions. (Skill)
- Students adhere to the professional code of ethics for pharmacy practice. (Value)
- Students value and respect the scientific approach to understanding natural phenomena. (Value)

29

Goals are too general to guide assessment and planning, so faculty develop learning objectives to make the goals explicit. Learning objectives operationalize program goals; they describe, in concrete terms, what program goals mean. Objectives should not be so specific that they are trivial, nor so general that they are vague. They describe observable behaviors that allow faculty to know if students have mastered the goals. For example, program learning objectives might state:

- Students can analyze experimental results and draw reasonable conclusions from them.

- Students can locate appropriate sources by searching electronic and print databases.

- Students can provide counseling services to people who are different from themselves in gender, age, ethnicity, culture, sexual orientation, or other significant characteristics.

- Students follow professional ethical standards when they provide nursing care to patients.

- Students can distinguish between science and pseudoscience.

DEVELOPING GOALS AND OBJECTIVES

Although the task of creating goals and objectives may appear simple, this process generally involves much spirited discussion about what faculty really want students to learn. Despite the potential for conflict, it is important that faculty participate in this discussion. By spending time collaborating on learning objectives, faculty refine their vision of the program and avoid later disagreements and misunderstandings. Program faculty might find it useful to appoint a small group to draft the goals and objectives, but eventually all faculty should participate in the discussion. Faculty who are not involved in determining goals and objectives are unlikely to be enthusiastic about using them for program improvement.

Sometimes faculty abdicate their role in developing program objectives. Department chairs may unilaterally develop the objectives, or this task may be shifted to a junior faculty member who has neither the authority nor the credibility to generate departmental buy-in. The program is "owned" by faculty, and they should decide what the program should accomplish and how to assess student progress. Creating a shared understanding of the mission, goals, and objectives forms the basis for curriculum design, assessment, and improvement. It is time well spent.

Consensus about mission, goals, and objectives does not always come easily. Most faculty have preference for and allegiance to particular aspects of their discipline, such as an emphasis on theoretical versus applied mathematics, intrapersonal versus interpersonal dynamics, or quantitative versus qualitative methodology. When program objectives are written, faculty must develop a broad overview of the whole program, and this presents challenges if the process creates conflicts among competing factions. Discussion at department meetings and retreats may require a skilled facilitator or even an outside consultant.

Consensus should be viewed as a process, not a result. Everyone has a fair opportunity to influence the collective decision, and the group seeks to maximize the input and support of all participants. If consensus is implemented effectively, all faculty feel they had an opportunity to present their views and affect results. Figure 2.1 provides suggestions for developing consensus that might be useful to the person who facilitates this discussion (Johnson & Johnson, 1997).

In addition to the usual dimensions of knowledge, skills, and values, faculty may want to consider other ways to categorize goals and objectives. For example, they might find it useful to separate institution-wide from discipline-specific goals (e.g., Allen, Noel, Deegan, Halpern, & Crawford, 2000). In the former category are a variety of general education goals, such as communication skills, critical thinking, and information literacy (see Figure 2.2). Although these goals are institution-wide, faculty might agree that their program helps students develop them beyond what is expected of all campus graduates. Sometimes campuses expect all academic programs to reinforce and build on campus-wide objectives, and programs may be required to include them among their learning goals. Program-specific goals might focus on student mastery of content, theory, methods, applications, ethics, and values within the discipline, as shown in Figure 2.2. Faculty also might consider students' long-term career development. For example, faculty at Kwantlen University College in British Columbia are encouraged to include "employability skills" among their goals, such as creative thinking, problem solving, teamwork, leadership, and intercultural skills (Macpherson, 2001).

FIGURE 2.1

SUGGESTIONS FOR ACHIEVING CONSENSUS

- Before the discussion begins, consider establishing ground rules that promote an open discussion and that encourage participants to be respectful if they disagree over issues.

- Encourage all participants to present their views and to explain the rationale for their opinions.

- Role model support for the airing of different viewpoints and repeatedly seek out differences of opinion by inviting everyone to contribute.

- Avoid a win-lose atmosphere. Instead, remind participants that the purpose is not to see whose ideas are the best, but to develop the best solution for the department as a whole.

- Avoid conflict-reducing techniques that prematurely terminate discussion, such as voting for each goal or objective separately.

- Regularly summarize positions in a fair way and seek common ground among them. Continue to question faculty about their reasons for supporting certain goals and objectives and not others.

- Once decisions appear to be agreed upon, check with all members to see if everyone can support the final selection of goals and objectives. If everyone supports the choices, you have reached consensus.

Faculty who have not yet developed their program goals and objectives don't have to start from scratch. They can save time by taking advantage of the work of others. Many campuses already have articulated goals and objectives. For example, George Mason University (http://assessment.gmu.edu/ProgramGoals/index.cfm) and the University of Colorado at Boulder (http://www.colorado.edu/pba/outcomes/units/unitindx.htm) list learning objectives for many of their academic programs. Professional organizations and specialized accrediting commissions often provide best practices guidelines, and many of these are readily available on the web. Each program is unique, so it makes sense to adapt what others have done, rather than to simply adopt their ideas.

One way to identify goals and objectives is to adopt a top-down approach based on analyzing documents that describe their program. Examples of such resources are catalogs, mission statements, program

---

FIGURE 2.2
POSSIBLE LEARNING GOALS

Institution-Wide Goals	Program Learning Goals
• Civic responsibility, values, and ethics. • Communication skills. • Critical thinking skills and habits. • Information literacy. • Intellectual flexibility. • Interpersonal and teamwork skills. • Knowledge integration across the disciplines. • Lifelong learning skills. • Multicultural understanding. • Problem-solving skills. • Quantitative skills.	• Understanding the theories, concepts, and research findings of the discipline. • Using appropriate methodologies to develop knowledge and to examine questions within the discipline. • Applying what was learned to relevant phenomena. • Being aware of ethical issues and adopting ethical standards within the discipline. • Being aware of and adopting major values that professionals within the discipline share.

---

brochures, and accreditation reports. Alternatively, a bottom-up approach might prove useful. Faculty could review instructional materials, such as syllabi, assignments, tests, and texts, looking for explicit or implicit expectations for knowledge, skills, and values that students are expected to develop.

Another way to uncover goals and objectives is for faculty to describe the ideal graduate of their program. What does this person know? What can this person do? What does this person care about? Faculty also might find it useful to ask for input from important stakeholders, such as students, alumni, and employers. What do they believe that students should know, do, and value by the end of the program? The answers are likely to contribute to the list of program goals and objectives.

Sometimes faculty are reluctant to include important objectives, such as being tolerant of others' viewpoints, because they are concerned that these intangible outcomes may not be assessable. Even though this may be a legitimate concern, it is important that faculty identify the objectives that are important to them. Most objectives can be assessed, including attitudes and values, although the assessment strategy may be something other than a traditional exam or survey. Chapters 5 and 6 describe a variety of strategies that are commonly used, and at least one of those strategies can be used to assess almost any educational objective. If faculty do not include their most important goals and objectives, assessment will be peripheral to their main interests and will be unlikely to result in meaningful assessment.

DEPTH OF PROCESSING

Creating objectives that specify the appropriate depth of processing is crucial for program and assessment planning. As faculty shift from describing what they cover to defining what students learn, they must determine what they mean by *learning*. Faculty want students to *know* the content, but they also want students to be able to *use* what they learn to solve problems and create new understanding. One of the most well-known descriptions of depth of processing is Bloom's (1956) taxonomy, and many find it useful for clarifying the desired level of performance (Krumme, 2002). The six levels described by Bloom are:

- Knowledge–To know specific facts, terms, concepts, principles, or theories.

- Comprehension–To understand, interpret, compare and contrast, explain.

- Application–To apply knowledge to new situations, to solve problems.

- Analysis–To identify the organizational structure of something; to identify parts, relationships, and organizing principles.

- Synthesis–To create something, to integrate ideas into a solution, to propose an action plan, to formulate a new classification scheme.

- Evaluation–To judge the quality of something based on its adequacy, value, logic, or use.

The depth of processing increases as we ask students to go beyond knowledge into comprehension, application, analysis, synthesis, and evaluation.

Many different objectives can be written for the same goal, and they can vary in depth of processing. For example, here are possible learning objectives at each of Bloom's levels for the following goal: "Students will understand the major theoretical approaches within the discipline."

- Students can list the major theoretical approaches of the discipline. (Knowledge)

- Students can describe the key theories, concepts, and issues for each of the major theoretical approaches. (Comprehension)

- Students can apply theoretical principles to solve real-world problems. (Application)

- Students can analyze the strengths and limitations of each of the major theoretical approaches for understanding specific phenomena. (Analysis)

- Students can combine theoretical approaches to explain complex phenomena. (Synthesis)

- Students can select the theoretical approach that is most applicable to a phenomenon and explain why they have selected that perspective. (Evaluation)

Faculty should consider different levels of performance and write their objectives to be consistent with the level of performance they desire.

Although Bloom's taxonomy is the most well-known, others point to the importance of promoting and assessing deep processing among our students. Biggs (1999) uses the concepts of deep versus surface learning to describe qualitatively different levels of understanding. Deep learning makes knowledge personal and relevant to real-world applications. Surface learning encourages superficial study strategies that rely on memorization and that do not lead to deeper understanding. He argues that the ways we teach, grade, and assess students influence whether they develop deep or surface learning. Wiggins (1998) agrees that understanding involves personalizing what is learned, such as relating it to one's experience and using it in ways that demonstrate "intellectual autonomy" (p. 39). Wiggins, like Biggs, expresses the concern that the ways we grade and assess student learning " . . . tend unwittingly to reinforce thoughtless mastery as an aim by failing to distinguish between 'thoughtful use' and 'correct answer' and by routinely valuing de facto the latter" (p. 207).

Most faculty abhor the thought that students might memorize isolated facts and concepts without developing the ability to use that knowledge; but teaching, grading, and assessment practices can promote the very surface learning that we want to avoid. Faculty interested in promoting deep learning should articulate this in program goals and objectives, design curricula and courses that give students the opportunity to develop these skills, and use grading and assessment strategies that provide students and faculty with formative feedback on development in the desired direction.

GUIDELINES FOR WRITING PROGRAM LEARNING OBJECTIVES

Learning objectives should be stated using active verbs that clearly communicate the depth of processing. Verbs that describe outcomes at different levels of Bloom's taxonomy are presented in Figure 2.3, and many faculty have found such lists helpful as they delineate objectives. For example, if faculty want students to be able to apply their knowledge, they can use the verbs apply, solve, interpret, or demonstrate. If they want students to demonstrate their attitudes or values, they might select verbs such as choose, decide, judge, or value. These verbs clarify the depth of processing and guide faculty as they examine the curriculum and develop assessment strategies.

Objectives also should clarify if faculty expectations are for absolute or value-added attainment. Is the major goal for students to improve or for them to reach some absolute level of performance? The language should make this clear: "Students will improve their ability to prove geometric theorems" versus "Students can prove geometric theorems." Most program learning objectives state absolute standards, but there are exceptions. For example, music programs often offer studio courses to support individual improvement of instrumental and vocal skills, and the relevant learning objectives have a value-added focus.

FIGURE 2.3
RELEVANT VERBS

Knowledge	Comprehension	Application	Analysis	Synthesis	Evaluation
cite	arrange	apply	analyze	arrange	appraise
define	classify	change	appraise	assemble	assess
describe	convert	compute	break down	categorize	choose
identify	describe	construct	calculate	collect	compare
indicate	defend	demonstrate	categorize	combine	conclude
know	diagram	discover	compare	compile	contrast
label	discuss	dramatize	contrast	compose	criticize
list	distinguish	employ	criticize	construct	decide
match	estimate	illustrate	debate	create	discriminate
memorize	explain	interpret	determine	design	estimate
name	extend	investigate	diagram	devise	evaluate
outline	generalize	manipulate	differentiate	explain	explain
recall	give examples	modify	discriminate	formulate	grade
recognize	infer	operate	distinguish	generate	interpret
record	locate	organize	examine	manage	judge
relate	outline	practice	experiment	modify	justify
repeat	paraphrase	predict	identify	organize	measure
reproduce	predict	prepare	illustrate	perform	rate
select	report	produce	infer	plan	relate
state	restate	schedule	inspect	prepare	revise
underline	review	shop	inventory	produce	score
	suggest	sketch	outline	propose	select
	summarize	solve	question	rearrange	summarize
	translate	translate	relate	reconstruct	support
		use	select	relate	value
			solve	reorganize	
			test	revise	

Adapted from Gronlund (1991).

Some experts suggest more detailed learning objectives. Mager (1997) recommends that objectives specify a behavior, a condition, and a criterion. For example, "Students can translate a Spanish newspaper into

37

English with no more than .2 errors per sentence." This specifies the behavior (create a translation), the condition (students are provided a Spanish newspaper), and the criterion (no more than .2 errors per sentence). In practice, it appears that this model is more useful for course learning objectives than for program learning objectives, and meaningful assessment can be conducted without this level of specificity. Performance criteria often are clarified during the assessment process. For example, faculty may develop a rubric describing different levels of student performance. Agreement on reasonable expectations emerges as they develop or apply the rubric or discuss results.

Effective program learning objectives should:

- Focus on the learner, not the teacher—on what students will learn, not on what faculty will teach.

- Explain how students can demonstrate mastery of program goals.

- Comprehensively define each goal.

- Use active verbs that specify definite, observable behaviors.

- Identify the depth of processing that faculty expect.

- Distinguish between absolute and value-added expectations.

Faculty also may invite students to review the objectives and identify any sources of ambiguity. The final result should be a set of clear, useful learning objectives that guide curriculum planning, teaching, learning, and assessment.

In this era of accountability, we no longer have the luxury of being vague about what we expect from our graduates. Not only does the assessment process demand clarity, but also students and the public deserve to know what they are getting in return for their money and time. Once faculty have clearly defined program objectives, they can determine whether their program provides the means for students to achieve them. Chapter 3 describes how to use program learning objectives to design curricula and courses to create a cohesive curriculum.

3

ALIGNMENT

As a whole, the educational experience should encourage, support, and reward students for mastering program learning objectives. We should develop and offer cohesive curricula that are systematically aligned with program objectives, and we should use objectives to plan course activities and grading schemes. Learning objectives guide curriculum planning and are the criteria for program success. "When taken seriously, assessment shapes curricula and instructional practice. The business community axiom that 'what gets measured, gets done' holds true in education as well" (Association of American Colleges and Universities, 2002, We Can Ensure Ongoing Improvement by . . . section, ¶ 7).

Alignment involves clarifying the relationship between what students do in their courses and what faculty expect them to learn. Here is a true story, and it is not unique. Faculty developed a set of learning objectives for their program, and among them was a statement that graduates should be able to write traditional term papers. They were surprised when they examined the curriculum. Faculty who used to assign term papers had substituted different types of writing assignments. They required students to write position papers, reflective essays, personal journals–everything except term papers. Faculty, working independently, had made good decisions for their courses, but they had assumed that others continued to assign term papers. Discussing the alignment between curriculum and objectives allowed them to identify this problem and find a solution. They agreed to reintroduce term papers in several required courses.

Faculty frequently identify gaps when they analyze the alignment between their curriculum and learning objectives, and they often make curricular changes to improve student learning opportunities *before* they even begin to collect program assessment data. This is why curricular alignment is an important component of program assessment. An interesting side effect of the curriculum alignment process often occurs. As faculty consider their own and others' contributions, they often develop increased appreciation for the complementary strengths of all department members. If program objectives are valued, then faculty who help students achieve these objectives are valued, too. For example, in some departments there are conflicts between theoretical and applied faculty; however, most faculty agree that students should develop both strengths. Faculty who specialize in one of these approaches often develop more respect for colleagues who specialize in the other approach when they recognize that complementary faculty strengths allow them to present a well-rounded curriculum. A typical comment goes something like this: "I used to think that Terry was dispensable, but now I'm really happy that Terry is in our department because I'd hate to have to teach those applied/methods/theoretical courses that our curriculum requires."

THE COHESIVE CURRICULUM

A cohesive curriculum systematically provides students opportunities to synthesize, practice, and develop increasingly complex ideas, skills, and values. Important learning objectives should be introduced early, and they should be reinforced and further developed throughout the curriculum (Diamond, 1997). For example, if faculty want students to develop writing skills, increasingly complex writing projects should be assigned. This is different from having a single "Engineering Writing 101" course in an engineering curriculum. Such courses are unlikely to have much long-term impact if the rest of the curriculum provides no reinforcement for writing. The same could be said for other core abilities that students should develop, such as oral communication, teamwork, and information competence skills. The distribution of content across the curriculum also is important. For example, are American literature majors more likely to develop an understanding of African-American literature if it is restricted to one required course or if it is spread throughout the curriculum? Aligning the curriculum with program objectives helps faculty address such questions.

Focusing on learning objectives allows faculty to evaluate and improve curricula and can lead to the development of new policies and procedures. Many examples of alignment projects are summarized in *Student Learning: A Central Focus for Institutions of Higher Education* (Doherty, Riordan, & Roth, 2002). Here are a few of their experiences:

- Faculty at the University of Alaska Southeast identified student writing as a major goal, and faculty from its three campuses (Juneau, Sitka, and Ketchikan) worked together to develop a common lower-division curriculum aligned with learning objectives and a set of rubrics to assess student writing portfolios. The process was eventually broadened to include the alignment of courses within majors to improve student writing throughout the curriculum and the examination of senior-level writing samples (Madden & Mulle, 2002).

- Faculty at Avila College examined the alignment of their curriculum with college-wide learning objectives. Responsibilities for teaching and assessing learning objectives were assigned to specific courses, procedures for certifying communication-intensive courses were developed, policies for embedding the assessment of higher-level thinking skills were enacted, and faculty development opportunities to increase faculty assessment expertise were offered to faculty and were integrated into new faculty orientations (Harris, 2002).

- Faculty at Bowling Green State University examined learning objectives for the majors and identified six "University Learning Outcomes" that were common to all programs. These are indicated by the verbs: "write, present, investigate, connect, participate, and lead" (Gromko & Hakel, 2002, p. 42). They noticed the need to better align general education and major expectations for student learning and to align courses with these objectives. Faculty are considering the use of common rubrics to assess these university-wide objectives (Gromko & Hakel, 2002).

41

- The B.A. program at the DePaul University School for New Learning is designed to meet 50 competence statements, and learning objectives are assigned to specific courses. Faculty are encouraged to develop appropriate pedagogy and assessment procedures, and the campus provides ongoing faculty development support for these activities, including an orientation for new faculty, ongoing mentoring, and a "core course handbook" with suggested assessment activities (McGury, 2002).

- Faculty in the Department of Mathematics/Computer Sciences at River College analyzed the alignment of their curriculum with their learning objectives and found the need to add a new capstone course, to better integrate learning objectives into syllabi and course planning, and to better integrate adjunct faculty into assessment activities. A follow-up analysis of syllabi verified improved use of course learning objectives (Cunningham, 2002).

- Faculty at the Rose-Hulman Institute of Technology use an electronic "curriculum map" that ties course objectives to campus-wide objectives. Campus-wide assessment data are analyzed to identify program-specific deficiencies, and program faculty use the curriculum map to identify where changes are needed (Rogers, Williams, & Misovich, 2002).

- Faculty in Truman State's Liberal Studies program developed learning objectives for their program, then built a new core curriculum based on courses specifically created or redesigned to align with these objectives. Faculty submitted course proposals which described how learning objectives would be developed and assessed, and a committee evaluated these proposals to decide which courses would be included (Christiansen, 2002).

ALIGNING CURRICULA WITH OBJECTIVES

An easy way to analyze the alignment between curricula and objectives is by organizing the data into matrices. Figure 3.1 is an alignment matrix for an undergraduate program with nine required courses and six learning objectives. Entries in such matrices can be simple check marks, or they can provide more information, as illustrated here. Take a few minutes to examine Figure 3.1 before reading the next paragraph. Does the curriculum appear cohesive?

The program summarized in Figure 3.1 appears to be well-aligned with Objectives 1 and 6. Both are introduced early, practiced in other courses, and demonstrated in upper-division work. The program, however, appears to have some problems with other objectives. Although Objective 2 is introduced, it is ignored in the rest of the curriculum; graduates are unlikely to retain the learning or develop sophistication in it. Objective 3 was never formally introduced. Perhaps this is not a problem if the introduction is known to occur in other coursework, such as general education classes. Objective 4 was not included in the curriculum. Faculty who teach the 490 course assume students have already had experience with Objective 5, but this has not been structured into program requirements. Faculty who are responsible for this program are in the best position to identify problems and find solutions. They also may decide to revisit their objectives and ask if some objectives, such as Objective 4, are worth retaining.

FIGURE 3.1
CURRICULUM ALIGNMENT MATRIX

Course	Program Objective 1	Program Objective 2	Program Objective 3	Program Objective 4	Program Objective 5	Program Objective 6
100	I					I
120		I				P
200	P		P			P
204						P
300	P		P			
329	D					P
400			P			D
480						
490	D		D		D	D

I = Introduced, P = Practiced, D = Demonstrated

43

ALIGNING COURSES WITH OBJECTIVES

Consider two faculty who are teaching a Shakespeare course for majors. One works on a campus in which most English majors will become high school teachers, and faculty agree that a priority objective for this course is to help students learn to stage Shakespeare's plays with high school actors. The other teaches in a department that places strong emphasis on understanding writing in its cultural context, and faculty agree that this course should be designed to help students understand the historical context underlying Shakespeare's works. These faculty will develop substantially different courses. Their students may read the same plays, but they will participate in different activities and will be graded based on different criteria.

Explicit course objectives guide course planning. "The idea is simple: one should have a clear idea of what the intended outcomes of the course are if one is to rationally develop it" (Menges, Weimer, & Associates, 1995, p. 188). Or, as the saying goes, "If you don't know where you're going, you're likely to end up someplace else." Having delineated objectives allows faculty to plan assignments, activities, and grading. For example, faculty might create a table with three columns (objective, activity, and assessment) that shows what students will learn, how the course will be structured to promote this learning, and how learning will be assessed. Figure 3.2 shows course planning entries for one objective. Notice the focus on what students will do to develop the competence and an explicit plan for giving feedback about their mastery when determining grades.

Course learning objectives are not secrets. Highlighting them on syllabi allows students to make informed decisions before enrolling, to monitor and direct their own learning, and to communicate what they have learned to others, such as graduate schools, employers, or transfer institutions. Explicitly tying course objectives to program objectives helps students recognize their involvement in a cohesive curriculum, and some assessment practices (such as portfolios) encourage students to monitor their progress throughout the curriculum. The Association of American Colleges and Universities (2002) promotes the development of students as *intentional* learners, and alignment efforts promote faculty as *intentional* teachers. The use of learning objectives contributes to these goals.

FIGURE 3.2
COURSE PLANNING GRID FOR ONE OBJECTIVE

Course Objective	Activity	Assessment
Students can write research reports in APA style.	• Students will work in groups to apply the APA style manual to a set of simulated research report sections created to include APA style violations. Whole-class discussion will ensure that all violations have been identified. • Students will conduct a research project and will iterate drafts of the sections of their research reports, based on peer feedback collected on checklists specifying APA style requirements.	• Objective exam questions on the second quiz and the final will examine student knowledge of APA style guidelines. • The grade for student research reports will include a measurement of conformity to APA style.

Figure 3.3 is an example of a matrix that could be used to examine course alignment with program objectives by relating course objectives to program objectives. Course objectives need not be identical to program objectives. For example, a program might specify that graduates will have a variety of laboratory skills, but a particular course might have only some of those skills among its objectives. As before, these matrices might contain only check marks, or they may contain more detailed information, such as the level of expectation for student mastery. Before reading the next paragraph, evaluate the course summarized in Figure 3.3, assuming that the program has only four learning objectives.

Taken out of context, it is difficult to evaluate this matrix. This appears to be a lower-division course in the major because its objectives tend to be at basic or intermediate levels of expectation. The course also appears to play an important role within the overall program because

FIGURE 3.3
COURSE ALIGNMENT MATRIX

	Program Objective 1	Program Objective 2	Program Objective 3	Program Objective 4
Course Objective 1	B			
Course Objective 2	B	B		
Course Objective 3		B		
Course Objective 4			I	
Course Objective 5			I	
Course Objective 6				
Course Objective 7				

B = Basic, I = Intermediate, A = Advanced expectation for this objective

three of the four program objectives are given attention. Program faculty, of course, are the best judges of this, and they may prefer that this course offer more extensive development of one or two program objectives, rather than split time among three of them. The faculty member has added two additional course objectives beyond program expectations, which is fine as long as students are given sufficient opportunity to develop the agreed-upon program objectives. Faculty advisors, aware of these added course objectives, can advise relevant students to take this section of the course, giving them opportunities to develop additional strengths.

This course alignment matrix maps details of each course's relationship to program objectives, allowing all program faculty to be aware of what individual courses contribute and providing information for discussion concerning where learning should occur.

FACULTY COLLABORATION AND AUTONOMY

Developing a cohesive curriculum should not threaten faculty control of their courses. Sections of required courses need not have identical syllabi and structure, and programs are strengthened if students are advised into course sections that match their individual needs. Basic, agreed-upon learning objectives should be included in each course, regardless of teacher and instructional mode, but faculty, of course, can supplement these basic objectives with personal objectives and can structure the course in different ways to promote student learning. Most faculty enjoy finding creative ways to motivate and contribute to their students, including sharing aspects of their disciplines that they find particularly exciting. Programs should capitalize on faculty strengths and encourage faculty to share what they love with students.

Agreeing on course learning objectives does not standardize courses. There are many ways to help students learn. For example, if an objective is for students to improve their ability to work in groups, groups could be given a variety of assignments and could be formed in many ways. Groups could meet face-to-face during class or outside of class, or virtual groups could be formed. One instructor may have a series of small group projects with groups varying in membership, while another may form collaborative groups that work together throughout the term. Feedback on group participation could be made by peers, self-evaluation, and/or faculty evaluation, and it could be structured using rating scales or rubrics. Similarly, if one of the course objectives is to improve student writing, students could write a variety of papers, review each other's writing, do collaborative writing, iterate drafts of papers, and/or critically examine writing samples. Individual faculty should find ways to meet learning objectives that are consistent with their own and their students' teaching and learning styles, and faculty who foster similar learning objectives should be encouraged to compare notes on the effectiveness of the strategies they employ.

ALIGNING TEACHING, GRADING, AND ASSESSMENT

Identifying specific learning objectives for programs and courses helps faculty focus on developing effective pedagogy for achieving these objectives. Here are some projects designed to align pedagogy with learning objectives:

- Faculty at Indiana University of Pennsylvania are invited to participate in the Reflective Practice Project in which they discuss and develop pedagogical approaches tied to specific learning objectives. Faculty participate in monthly workshops, interdisciplinary teaching circles, departmental teaching circles, and two annual Saturday workshops featuring nationally recognized pedagogy experts. This program helps faculty develop a repertoire of teaching approaches so they can customize course activities for particular needs. Faculty in some programs, such as chemistry, have coordinated their teaching to systematically focus on the development of their students across the curriculum (Cessna, 2002).

- The mission of Niagara University includes commitments to serve the poor and to learn through service, and their general education learning objectives specify that "students become committed, dedicated members of their society and seek to serve others" (Baxter, 2002, p. 85). To align their courses with this mission and objective, faculty routinely include community service. For example, accounting students help senior citizens and disadvantaged people fill out tax forms, and they participate in class discussions of what they learned from such experiences. Students in a senior-level literature course read novels about people living in poverty, and they are required to volunteer for about 20 hours at a local parenting center that serves underprivileged families. At the end of the semester, students publicly share reflections relating their readings to the reality of the families they served, and students "regularly comment that the experience was a life transforming one" (Baxter, 2002, p. 86).

- Faculty at North Carolina State University are invited to participate in their grant-funded inquiry-guided learning project. Students in inquiry-guided courses learn through solving problems that have multiple answers. Efforts target four learning goals: "critical thinking, independent inquiry, intellectual development and maturity, and student responsibility for learning" (Lee, 2002, p. 89). Faculty, staff, and administrators jointly focus on these goals, providing students with a cohesive environment that helps them master discipline-based, as well as project-based learning objectives (Lee, 2002).

- Faculty at Samford University have adopted a problem-based learning (PBL) approach to teaching, and courses are organized around a series of complex problems that students address. Problems are selected that lead students toward the mastery of relevant learning objectives, and many faculty have developed authentic measures to assess this learning. Chapman (2002) reports that using a PBL approach helps improve faculty focus on what students do and what students learn, reducing their emphasis on content coverage and increasing their emphasis on developing student skills to produce, rather than consume, knowledge.

- Faculty at the College of William and Mary defined campus-wide objectives for "digital information literacy" with three major foci: knowledge generation, knowledge access, and knowledge evaluation. They developed web-based tutorials targeting these objectives and embedded assessment within the teaching modules. Students learn about technology by using technology, and assessments allow students who enter with strong technical skills to quickly complete modules, rather than spend time "learning" skills they already have (College of William and Mary, 2002).

- Faculty in nearly two-thirds of the programs at the University of Wisconsin-La Crosse have targeted student writing by participating in their writing-in-the-major project. Rather than rely on composition faculty to develop student writing, program faculty work together to develop a cohesive curriculum that systematically develops writing skills within the major. Program faculty agree on learning objectives for student writing, plan a developmental approach for teaching writing, and use assessment data to improve the pedagogy (Cerbin & Beck, 2002).

Aligning teaching and grading with course objectives reinforces the alignment of program objectives with the curriculum, promotes student development in agreed-upon directions, and provides opportunities for embedded assessment. For example, faculty could agree to embed some common questions in course exams to assess mastery of both course and program objectives.

Exams which challenge students should be in courses that provide students opportunities to meet these high expectations. If learning objectives focus on deep learning and higher levels of Bloom's taxonomy, students should practice this depth during course activities, and assignments and exams should require the demonstration of this depth. Grading is a powerful tool for motivating and directing student learning (McKeachie, 1999). If exams focus on simple regurgitation of facts, students will focus on acquiring facts; but if exams focus on deep processing, students will change what they learn.

Douglas Eder, director of undergraduate assessment and program review at Southern Illinois University Edwardsville (SIUE), advocates the integration of assessment and teaching (Eder, 2001). He offers the flight simulator as a model for this activity. Student pilots spend hours in flight simulators, and they learn by responding to simulated catastrophes, "crashing" planes in a safe environment without risk to themselves or passengers. They can repeatedly deal with real-world situations faced by professional pilots, and teaching and assessment are inseparable because the feedback and the opportunity to try again are instantaneous and unambiguous. Eder encourages faculty to embed the equivalent of flight simulators in their classes and to use these authentic activities to teach as well as assess student learning.

SIUE faculty in many disciplines have developed the equivalent of the flight simulator by integrating a Senior Assignment into their programs (Eder, 2001). Senior majors create a product (e.g., a thesis, essay, or performance) under the supervision of a faculty member, and then present this product to the appropriate audience (e.g., faculty, peers, agencies, or the general public). Students learn while developing these projects, and their ability to integrate learning from previous courses can be assessed as products are developed, refined, and presented.

Faculty have become accustomed to traditional tests, but many have become more interested in using authentic assessments when learning objectives specify deep learning. Eder's suggestion that faculty embed safe opportunities to apply what is being learned promotes deep learning and provides embedded assessment data. This approach is similar to the classic apprenticeship model for teaching skilled trades and for mentoring graduate students. Students learn while creating products under the supervision of expert mentors, and the proof of their learning is in the quality of their products and their ability to explain and defend them. Opportunities to use these products for program assessment abound.

Wiggins (1998) provides other examples similar to the flight simulator: Students in teacher education interact with simulated and real students in mentored classrooms, and music students participate in bands and orchestras. Similarly, art, business, ethics, journalism, nursing, pharmacy, and psychology students analyze real-word cases and do internships in museums, corporations, and health centers.

Embedded assessment allows activities to serve multiple functions and can provide effective grading and assessment data. Participating faculty often develop improved understanding of program objectives as they collaborate on embedded assessment projects. Embedded assessments make good use of what students and faculty already do, making assessment a part of the department's normal operations, rather than an extra task. Last, and most relevant to this chapter, embedding assessments can lead to more cohesive curricula because faculty work together to focus on program objectives when planning and implementing embedded assessment projects. Faculty already spend a great deal of time examining student learning, and embedding assessment allows these efforts to also serve program assessment purposes.

ALIGNING STUDENT
SERVICES TO SUPPORT LEARNING

Important faculty advising and mentoring roles often occur outside of the formal curriculum, and faculty are not the only ones who contribute

51

to student development (American College Personnel Association, 1996). Imagine being admitted to a hospital in which doctors, nurses, lab technicians, pharmacists, food service personnel, and other staff don't communicate about patient care. They aren't aware of what each other is doing, and they don't attempt to coordinate their services or examine their impact on patient health. We would not opt for this type of health care. Similarly, colleges and universities should provide coordinated support for student learning–in and out of the classroom (Maki, 2002a). Diamond (1997) expresses this well:

> . . . what goes on in the classroom is only a part of the total instructional experience of our students. No matter how effective we are as teachers and how well designed our courses and curricula are, we will not be successful if our libraries and residence halls are not conducive to studying, if student advisers and counselors provide our students with little personal support, if few opportunities for recreation exist, and if we, as faculty, are rarely available to meet with students outside of the classroom, laboratory, or studio. . . . A total educational program must be nurtured and planned by involving the staff from the offices of student affairs and residential life, among others. (p. 14)

Faculty, administrators, student support professionals, clerical and technical staff, and others should collaborate to support student achievement. An analysis of how campuses actually function suggests a lot of room for improvement (AAHE, ACPA, & NASPA, 1998). A *cohesive campus* should support faculty efforts, and other campus divisions should examine their impact on student development (Maki, 2002a). In this way, campuses examine their institutional effectiveness. Publications on the assessment of student affairs programs are available to assist campuses in this enterprise (e.g., Bauer & Hanson, 2001; Malaney, 1999; Upcraft & Schuh, 1996), and a balanced perspective on their impact would benefit from input from program assessment efforts.

The Policy Center for the First Year of College maintains an active listserv and web site to connect campus leaders who coordinate and assess freshmen programs (http://www.brevard.edu/fyc/listserv/index.htm). Gardner (2000) suggests that campuses examine their freshman experience "as a forest, rather than the trees" (¶ 4), and Cuseo (2002) suggests that they put this advice into practice by assessing the impact of new student orientations, advising, curricula, the co-curriculum (e.g., recreational and athletics programs), academic support programs (e.g., the library and tutoring center), and personal support programs (e.g., counseling and health services). Program faculty can profit from this advice when they do program assessment—they can examine overall campus and department support for their students in addition to examining how well students have mastered program learning objectives, and they can work among themselves and with other campus professionals to improve the educational environment for their students. Many of the indirect assessment techniques described in Chapter 6 are particularly useful for this task.

Alignment is not just a concept for faculty. A joint committee of the American Association of Higher Education, the American College Personnel Association, and the National Association of Student Personnel Administrators (1998) calls on college and university leaders to align all campus operations to promote student learning. They ask that:

> administrative leaders rethink the conventional organiza-
> tion of colleges and universities to create more inventive
> structures and processes that integrate academic and stu-
> dent affairs; align institutional planning, hiring, rewards,
> and resource allocations with the learning mission; offer
> professional development opportunities for people to coop-
> erate across institutional boundaries; use evidence of stu-
> dent learning to guide program improvement, planning and
> resource allocation; and communicate information on stu-
> dents' life circumstances and culture to all members of the
> college or university community. (¶ 5)

This is no small task! Program assessment is one part of some major changes occurring in higher education, and it contributes to our understanding of campus-wide educational effectiveness.

4

ASSESSMENT PLANNING AND
IMPLEMENTATION

C hapter 1 outlined six steps in an assessment program: develop learning objectives, check for program alignment, develop an assessment plan, collect data, use results, and examine assessment processes. Chapters 2 and 3 focused on the first two steps, and this chapter describes the third step, developing an assessment plan. Implementing this plan should contribute to the refinement of the program and should satisfy external demands for a quality assurance process.

Just as it takes time for faculty to define program learning objectives and align the curriculum with those objectives, it takes time to develop an assessment plan. Some campuses require formal assessment plans that are subject to review and approval by relevant administrators or committees, and others have less formal procedures. Developing an assessment plan should save faculty time, in the long run, because it should help them avoid false starts and ill-fated projects.

The assessment process should be meaningful, manageable, and sustainable. Faculty time is valuable and should be spent on assessment activities that target important learning objectives and that are likely to improve student learning. If faculty try to assess all the program objectives at once, they may find themselves *data rich* and *information poor.* Instead, faculty could plan a series of smaller, more manageable assessment projects. A good way to begin is by assessing one or two objectives that faculty are fairly confident their students are mastering. Results that confirm faculty beliefs will be good news and will help the department begin their assessment program by demonstrating some important successes.

Assessment studies take time and money, so the assessment plan must be reasonable in scope. If the plan is not manageable, it is likely to generate hostility and abandonment. Assessment is an ongoing process, not a one-shot or periodic effort, and the plan should define a multiyear program that eventually examines all learning objectives. Scalability is of concern if enrollments are increasing. For example, portfolios may be excellent for small programs, but the portfolio process may become overwhelming if the program grows. If the plan becomes unmanageable or if the process becomes trivialized, assessment will be neither effective nor sustainable. Faculty should conclude that assessment provides them value that exceeds the cost of their time and effort.

One of the most important aspects of program assessment is that faculty discuss student learning, and these discussions naturally include consideration of curriculum, pedagogy, and student support services. Assessment focuses attention on helping students master learning objectives, and this learner-centered approach involves curriculum and course alignment and collaboration with staff who support student development. Focusing on the learning objectives provides common goals for all campus professionals.

Quality assurance processes should base decision-making on evidence, and that evidence should include reliable, valid assessments of student learning. Programs cannot declare themselves educationally effective by pointing at the degrees that faculty hold, the quality of the computer facilities, or the occasional alumnus who is exceptionally successful. Faculty assess programs by collecting empirical evidence to examine student learning, and they rely on this evidence to guide decision-making. Faculty reflect on what they learn from assessment studies, confirm when students are successfully mastering objectives, and develop appropriate strategies to respond to identified deficiencies.

Assessment should lead to incremental improvements in the program, and these should be documented in a written record. If written records are not maintained, faculty are likely to lose track of the assessment program, forget what has been learned, and fail to follow through on agreed-upon changes. Many campuses require programs to submit an annual report on what was done, what was learned, and what impact the assessment had on program functioning (e.g., California State University, San Bernardino, 2002). This allows key personnel to track progress and to document the implementation of assessment to satisfy accreditation demands. Preparing for accreditation reviews becomes easier because the record of ongoing assessment speaks for itself.

The assessment plan should include the examination of the assessment process. Campus and program missions change, and these changes may require revisions to program objectives and assessment plans. In addition, experience gained while implementing the plan might lead faculty to reconsider their direction. A selected assessment strategy may not prove effective, a more promising one might be identified, or results might lead to questions that require further examination. The assessment plan should be flexible. Faculty should not feel locked in to an assessment process that is not working well or that fails to address important questions that emerge.

Those who create and implement the assessment plan have professional obligations to engage in ethical data collection and to respect those who provide data. Assessment processes that demean students, violate their confidences, invade their privacy, or make unreasonable demands on them are not appropriate and may generate reactions that undermine student-faculty relations and the quality of the assessment process. Faculty who engage in assessment should role model professional, ethical behavior to the students, alumni, and others who contribute needed information.

COMPONENTS OF AN ASSESSMENT PLAN

The assessment plan should explain "who is going to do what, when they will do it, and how they will use the information that is generated" (Palomba & Banta, 1999, p. 46). An easy way to organize an assessment plan is to create a matrix that lists the learning objectives in the first column. Subsequent columns would describe how each objective is aligned with the curriculum, how each will be assessed, when and how often each will be assessed, and who will be involved. Entries in the second column identify courses and other aspects of the curriculum that help students master each objective, and they document and formalize the alignment process described in the previous chapter. Once the plan is implemented, faculty might decide to add a column that summarizes what was learned about each objective and the impact of these findings, establishing a simple, written record of assessment activities.

A variety of assessment plans are available on the web, such as the academic program assessment plans at California State University, Sacramento (http://www.csus.edu/acaf/assmnt.htm) and assessment plans for a variety of academic and nonacademic programs at Dixie State University (http://www.dixie.edu/effective/outcomes.htm#hum). Reviewing some of these plans might make the task of developing your own easier.

SELECTING ASSESSMENT STRATEGIES

Program assessment studies primarily focus on how well students have mastered the program's learning objectives. Carefully worded objectives that specify the desired depth of processing and that clarify if objectives are for value-added or absolute attainment simplify this task. Faculty may have to revisit and revise their objectives if they lack sufficient clarity, are out-of-date, or have not been agreed upon by the faculty who coordinate and staff the program.

Although it is tempting to select an assessment strategy simply because it is readily available, it is more important to choose a strategy that will result in unambiguous assessment of the relevant learning objective. For example, assessing whether students can pass a standardized test or replicate a laboratory experiment serves little purpose if these tasks are unrelated to your program objectives. No one wants to spend the time and effort on assessment only to discover that results provide no useful feedback about the program.

Chapters 5 and 6 describe a variety of assessment strategies. Different strategies can provide complementary views of the program, and faculty should base assessment decisions on more than one source of information. Direct assessment, such as analyzing student projects to measure their mastery of a specific learning objective, can make a compelling case for whether students have achieved that objective. Assessment results will be even more convincing if different assessment strategies triangulate to support the same conclusions.

Indirect strategies for assessing student learning can supplement and enrich what faculty learn from direct assessment studies. Indirect strategies, such as surveys, can ask students to report how well they have met program objectives. Their perceptions, regardless of their accuracy, are important. A more typical use of indirect strategies, however, is to obtain other types of information about the program and its support for student learning. For example, faculty may be interested in student perceptions concerning the quality of program mentoring or advising, the usefulness of laboratory or computer facilities, the effectiveness of campus tutoring centers, or the value of relevant student organizations. These are not learning objectives, but they might make important contributions to student development. In addition, indirect evidence from alumni and employers can provide important information about the long-term impact of the program and can identify their suggestions for change.

Assessment techniques vary in their demands on faculty time and department resources, the need for outside support, and their credibility with faculty. Faculty should have confidence in the selected strategies. They may be asked to help collect and analyze data, and they should be willing to use the results for program improvement.

ESTABLISHING A CONTEXT FOR ASSESSMENT

A reasonable place to examine learning is where students normally demonstrate their learning–in courses. Assignments and exam questions can be created specifically to target program learning objectives, and students' work can be used for course grading *and* for program assessment. For example, faculty who teach senior-level courses could agree to embed an exam question that requires the application of ethical standards, and student responses to those questions could be accumulated across sections. The analysis of these data can lead to general conclusions about student mastery of relevant learning objectives.

Capstone courses are obvious places to embed assessment. Program faculty could require students to finalize and submit portfolios in the capstone course, including it as a graded assignment. Students in many programs complete senior projects, and assignments for these projects can focus on specific learning objectives, such as the integration of learning to solve real-world problems or to explain complex phenomena. These projects also could be examined as writing samples, and faculty might elect to analyze writing, critical thinking, and information competence skills. If oral communication is a program objective, faculty might require students to orally present senior projects. These activities could be organized into a Senior Presentation Day or other event. Faculty could assess relevant learning objectives, and community professionals could be invited to contribute to the assessment effort. This event could promote and celebrate student learning, provide a context for important discussion between faculty and students, help students network with community professionals, and serve program assessment purposes.

Students in some programs engage in community service learning, fieldwork, or internship experiences, and this presents another easy opportunity to include the judgments of community professionals in program assessment. Community supervisors could be asked to evaluate a variety of program learning objectives, such as communication skills, observance of ethical standards, and the ability to apply the discipline to real-world problems.

Some campuses and programs routinely ask students to participate in exit interviews or exit surveys as they are about to graduate. Questions that collect information on the mastery of learning objectives or that ask students to address other important issues could be included in these procedures, and data could be analyzed at the program and/or campus level, depending on what is being assessed.

Faculty may decide to use an assessment center (e.g., Riggio, Aguirre, Mayes, Belloli, & Kubiak, 1997; Zlatic, 2001). Assessment center staff generally use a variety of techniques to assess an array of objectives, and students may spend hours or days being assessed. Classic business tests, such as the In-Basket Test (students are required to cope with a simulated in-basket of real-world problems) and the Leaderless Group Discussion (students are rated on various dimensions related to their participation), could be combined with interviews and paper-and-pencil tests. Students could be tested when they enter the program and when they graduate to assess value-added components of their education, and preliminary results could be used to advise students about their choice of courses and program options (e.g., Kottke & Schultz, 1997).

Faculty who develop the assessment plan also should identify opportunities to piggyback on other campus assessment efforts. For example, some campuses have exit exams in which students must demonstrate writing skills, and these documents could be used to examine campus-wide and program-specific learning objectives associated with writing. Students have to write about *something*, and the writing assignment could be designed to assess other learning objectives. For example, the writing assignment might require students to demonstrate critical thinking skills or their understanding of historical, global, or multicultural issues.

Campuses are likely to have assessment plans for other general education requirements, and most programs have a variety of broad learning objectives that overlap with these campus-wide objectives. By working together, program faculty and faculty who are involved in the assessment of general education can avoid duplicating efforts. Data can be analyzed for each program separately, and they can be aggregated to reach conclusions about campus-wide learning.

Institutional research offices exist on most campuses, and their staff generally coordinate campus-wide surveys and other assessments. Faculty developing a program assessment plan may be able to use program-specific results from these efforts. For example, incoming students often have test scores that could be tracked to examine trends in the student population or that could be examined to uncover relationships important to advisors. Transcripts might provide useful information about the relative success of transfer and native students, of students who transfer from different institutions, of students who take traditional or online versions of courses, or of students who complete courses in different orders. An analysis might demonstrate that students do better in research methods courses if they have already completed core, lower-division general education courses, and such information might lead to restructuring prerequisites within the curriculum. Faculty who create the assessment plan should not get carried away with preexisting data bases, such as transcripts, but should consider framing specific questions that are of sufficient importance that they are worth pursuing.

RELIABILITY AND VALIDITY

Assessment results should be trustworthy, and a traditional way to examine this is to ask if results are *reliable* and *valid* (Allen & Yen, 2002). Reliability refers to measurement precision and stability, and reliability can be examined in a number of ways (see Figure 4.1). Conclusions about individuals are consistent when measurements are reliable. Reliability often is summarized with a correlation coefficient. If results are determined at random, the reliability coefficient is zero; and if identical results are obtained each time individuals are assessed, the reliability is 1.0. No procedure is perfectly reliable, but longer tests tend to be more reliable than shorter tests, procedures that assess abilities tend to be more reliable than ones that assess opinions or personalities, and objectively scored procedures tend to be more reliable than subjectively scored procedures.

Validity refers to how well a procedure assesses what it is supposed to be assessing. A valid assessment of a learning objective tells us how well students have mastered that objective, and it should provide useful for-

FIGURE 4.1
MAJOR TYPES OF RELIABILITY

Test-retest reliability	A reliability estimate based on assessing a group of people twice and correlating the two scores. This coefficient measures score stability.
Parallel forms reliability (or alternate forms reliability)	A reliability estimate based on correlating scores collected using two versions of the procedure. This coefficient indicates score consistency across the alternative versions.
Inter-rater reliability	How well two or more raters agree when decisions are based on subjective judgments.
Internal consistency reliability	A reliability estimate based on how highly parts of a test correlate with each other.
Coefficient alpha	An internal consistency reliability estimate based on correlations among all items on a test.
Split-half reliability	An internal consistency reliability estimate based on correlating two scores, each calculated on half of a test.

mative information. Figure 4.2 describes some major ways to evaluate a procedure's validity. Valid procedures avoid *bias*; that is, systematic underestimates or overestimates of what is being assessed. Bias and unreliability undermine validity because results are less trustworthy. Formative validity (i.e., how well the procedure yields findings that are useful for improving what is being assessed) is of primary importance for program assessment.

Reliability and validity are sometimes confused, but an absurd example should help clarify the difference. Imagine that we measure adult information literacy by multiplying people's head circumferences by 10.

FIGURE 4.2 MAJOR TYPES OF VALIDITY	
Construct validity	Construct validity is examined by testing predictions based on the theory (or construct) underlying the procedure. For example, faculty might predict that scores on a test that assesses knowledge of anthropological terms will increase as anthropology students progress in their major. We have more confidence in the test's construct validity if predictions are empirically supported.
Criterion-related validity	Criterion-related validity indicates how well results predict a phenomenon of interest, and it is based on correlating assessment results with this criterion. For example, scores on an admissions test can be correlated with college GPA to demonstrate criterion-related validity.
Face validity	Face validity is assessed by subjective evaluation of the measurement procedure. This evaluation may be made by test takers or by experts in what is being assessed.
Formative validity	Formative validity is how well an assessment procedure provides information that is useful for improving what is being assessed.
Sampling validity	Sampling validity is how well the procedure's components, such as test items, reflect the full range of what is being assessed. For example, a valid test of content mastery should assess information across the entire content area, not just isolated segments.

Using this procedure, a person with a head circumference of 25 inches has an information literacy score of 250, and the procedure awards higher scores to people with larger heads. Is this procedure reliable and valid? Adult head sizes are stable; and tape measures, properly applied, provide precise measurements. The assessment process is reliable because people receive the same score each time they're assessed. The obvious problem with this procedure is its validity. Adult head circumference tells us nothing about information literacy. We conclude that this procedure is reliable, but not valid. Faculty should avoid using procedures just because they are known to be reliable. Validity is crucial for program assessment.

ETHICAL ASSESSMENT

Faculty who conduct assessment projects generally examine student products or opinions, and they also may analyze responses from other individuals, such as alumni or employers. We have a professional responsibility to behave ethically any time we collect information from people, and we want to model ethical behavior within the communities we serve. In addition, valid assessment often requires the honest cooperation of respondents, and this is more likely to occur when we treat them with respect.

Campuses that receive federal grants are required to have a Human Subjects Institutional Review Board (HSIRB) which reviews research proposals before projects can be implemented (National Institutes of Health, 2001). Federal guidelines identify several categories of proposals, ranging from those that are exempt from review to those that require extensive review. For example, research involving children or the mentally ill requires extensive review because these populations are less able to make decisions to protect their own best interest. Most assessment studies would fall into the exempt category because research that is designed with the sole purpose of improving educational institutions is exempt. Assessment projects which also might result in publication or presentation at professional conferences fall into a gray area because they serve research as well as formative assessment purposes. Faculty should discuss such projects with their HSIRB to determine the appropriate level of review. If your campus does not have an HSIRB, you might like to consider establishing one that focuses on all human research or that focuses only on assessment studies.

Although explicit ethical principles have not yet been developed for program assessment, a number of professional organizations have developed guidelines for interactions with students, clients, and others:

- 9 *Principles of Good Practice for Assessing Student Learning* (AAHE, 1996)

- *Ethical Standards of AERA* (American Educational Research Association, 1992)

- *Code of Ethics for Institutional Research* (Association for Institutional Research, 2001)

- *Protection of Human Subjects in Research* (U.S. Department of Education, 2002)

- *The Belmont Report: Ethical Principles and Guidelines for the Protection of Human Subjects of Research* (National Commission for the Protection of Human Subjects of Biomedical and Behavioral Research, 1979)

- *Code of Professional Responsibilities in Educational Measurement* (National Council on Measurement in Education, 1995)

The Belmont Report (National Commission for the Protection of Human Subjects of Biomedical and Behavior Research, 1979) encouraged a risk-benefit approach to evaluate projects. Projects are acceptable if benefits outweigh risks and if risks are minimized or eliminated. Potential risks to participants in assessment studies include the possibility of divulging sensitive information, embarrassment, and possible retribution for critical feedback. In addition, the assessment procedure often makes demands on their time. On the other hand, program assessment has the potential to provide significant benefit to the program, university, and current and future students.

One of the most important rights of participants in human subjects research is respect for their autonomy. We should provide potential participants enough information about an assessment project for them to make an informed decision about their participation. This is why the concept of *informed consent* is so important in ethical codes–without informed consent, participants cannot exercise autonomy. Embedded assessment, a strategy that has many strengths, is sometimes used without securing informed consent. Faculty assume that there is no harm done because they plan to remove identifying information from student products before they are assessed. An easy solution is for instructors to inform students in advance that certain assignments may be used for grading *and* for assessment, and to ask students to indicate if they agree to this. Students rarely object to the use of their data for this purpose, and they may appreciate the demonstration of faculty respect for their autonomy.

Informed consent can prevent many issues from surfacing and create an atmosphere of respect that nourishes honest participation. By informing students about the purpose of the study, the uses of the data, and their rights as participants, faculty increase the likelihood that students will take the project seriously. Similarly, by establishing clear guidelines with colleagues, faculty who manage assessment projects can avoid being put in difficult situations, such as being asked to allow others to see students' names. We should be concerned about the ethical treatment of students, as well as the ethical treatment of each other. For example, faculty who collect data in their courses may be concerned that data will be used to reflect on their competence, rather than on student learning.

Figure 4.3 summarizes a number of ethical principles for the collection and use of human subject data, adapted to program assessment. Although all the concepts in this figure may not be applicable to every situation, professionals should be aware of them; should discuss them with colleagues when planning and conducting assessment studies; and should seek guidance from others, such as HSIRB members, when conclusions are problematic.

Several of these concepts apply to the use of data. Generally, we respect anonymity, confidentiality, and privacy. Data are *anonymous* if they cannot be associated with respondents, and they are *confidential* if they could be associated with respondents, but are not. For example, surveys often are anonymous because they do not include identifying information. On the other hand, focus group participants are known, but data are confidential if their identities are not disclosed. In most cases confidentiality can be achieved by preventing identifying information from being attached to data or, if this is not feasible, by expunging identi-

FIGURE 4.3
SELECTED ETHICAL CONCEPTS

Anonymity	The identify of participants in assessment studies is not recorded or is recorded in such a way that data elements cannot be associated with individuals.
Autonomy	Participants in assessment studies have the right to self-determination and to make decisions about participation without undue pressure that would reduce this right.
Beneficence	The assessment study is designed to maximize possible benefits and to minimize or eliminate possible harm.
Competence	Faculty are competent in the methodologies they use. When lacking formal training or experience with a method, faculty should seek appropriate training or assistance.
Confidentiality	The person who conducts the assessment study is aware of who participated, but does not disclose this information.
Data ownership	Faculty determine who has control over the assessment data-who has the right to see the data or to allow others to see them.
Data security	The security of assessment data and other information that could lead to the disclosure of confidential information is preserved.
Deception	Deception involves giving incorrect or misleading information to participants. It is difficult to imagine an assessment study that requires deception.
Disclosure of rights	Faculty inform potential participants of their rights, such as their right not to participate and to know the degree of confidentiality associated with their responses.
Dual relationships	Dual relationships exist when participants in assessment projects have more than one relationship to the person collecting or analyzing the data, such as student-teacher or employee-employer relationships. Having two or more roles can create competing expectations that may bias results, threaten objectivity, and lead to harm. For example, student participants may be subtly penalized for honest but critical statements.
Exploitation	Exploitation involves taking advantage of people over whom one has authority, such as students, supervisees, employees, and research participants. Participants in assessment studies should not be exploited.

(continued on page 68)

Fair and accurate	Assessment reports are based on data, not on the assessor's desires, biases, or other factors extrinsic to the assessment process.
Harm	Avoiding the risk of physical or emotional/psychological harm is a primary principle in the ethical guidelines of most organizations (e.g., American Psychological Association, 1992), and assessment studies should be reconsidered if collecting the data or reporting the results might harm participants.
Informed consent	Participants agree to participate in assessment projects, and this agreement is based on knowing the purpose of the project, the expected use of the data, the rights to not participate and to discontinue participation, and if data will be anonymous or confidential.
Justice	Participants in assessment projects are selected fairly and without placing an undue burden on them.
Negotiating an agreement	Principals agree in advance about the purposes of the project, the expected date of completion, ownership of the data, and who is to receive the report. If an external consultant, such as a staff member from an assessment center, is conducting the assessment, the "client," e.g., the department chair, should be clearly established, and results should be provided only to the "client."
Objectivity	Faculty have an unbiased attitude throughout the assessment process, including gathering evidence, interpreting evidence, and reporting the results.
Privacy	Participants have the right to determine what personal information they disclose in assessment studies. This includes the right to choose to skip questions that they prefer not to answer.

fying information from assessment reports, typically by aggregating data. Respect for privacy usually is demonstrated during the informed consent process when potential participants are told that they may decline to participate in the whole project or in any part of it.

Confidentiality concerns extend to the security of any data or records collected during assessment projects. Participants and faculty usually should not be identified in connection with the assessment data or reports at any point in the assessment process, although exceptions can exist, such as in some cases of embedded assessment and the use of portfolios. Other issues concerning the data are data ownership and security. It is important that faculty clarify who controls access to the data and how data will be stored to protect respondents. This includes the storage of data in a secure environment and the deletion or destruction of confidential data files and records when no longer needed.

Figure 4.4 presents a number of problematic ethical situations that may arise in program assessment, with analyses based on the ethical principles described above. You may not agree with the presented analyses, and you are encouraged to discuss these situations with colleagues, students, and your campus HSIRB. It is better to resolve ethical dilemmas *before* assessments are conducted, rather than after. For example, the University of Saskatchewan (1999) developed templates for assessment surveys and obtained blanket HSIRB approval for their use within specified guidelines. Assessment activities should not be conducted as if we have *carte blanche* to do whatever we want. To do so violates the trust of our students and invites reactions and restrictions that can undermine our ability to conduct effective assessments.

FIGURE 4.4
POTENTIAL ETHICAL SITUATIONS IN ASSESSMENT

- John is a student in a senior-level course who is told to go to a room to participate in a focus group on the geology program. John asks if he has to participate in the session, and the instructor informs him that it is during class time and therefore he must participate. Reluctantly, John joins the focus group.

Analysis: This is an assessment activity, not a class activity, and John should be given the right to decline. Instructors who properly inform students about the process will have few students opt out of such activities.

- Eva is in the nursing program. During a focus group in which confidentiality was promised, she mentioned some problems with advising, particularly with the transfer of credit from a foreign university. During her next advising session, her advisor expresses her disappointment with Eva for not coming to her directly about the transfer issue and invites Eva to switch to another advisor. Eva is upset because she did not want her response to undermine her relationship with her advisor.

Analysis: This should not have happened because Eva was promised confidentiality. The information was "leaked" and the process led to harm, violating at least two ethical principles.

(continued on page 70)

- Dr. Simpson is the only instructor of the methods class in anthropology. An assessment survey provided data that indicated students' displeasure with the methods class, and many students commented that the instructor needed to "learn how to teach." The report did not mention Dr. Simpson by name, but everyone knows that he is the only instructor. Because of the student comments, he was asked to teach a different class.

Analysis: This is a difficult issue that should be handled before the assessment is conducted by obtaining faculty understanding about the type of information that could be obtained. If this is done, and the primary purpose of the assessment is to honestly report information to improve the program, then information about this course is appropriate. It is possible that the problem is with the course, rather than with the instructor, and the program coordinator could respond to these results discreetly without causing anyone public embarrassment. The aphorism "praise in public and correct in private" is applicable to this situation.

- Students in the English program are required to submit a portfolio with evidence of having satisfied departmental program objectives. They also must write a critique of each of the classes they have taken. The portfolio is read by most of the faculty, and they are able to view these student comments about their classes.

Analysis: This strategy has the potential to harm students, especially those who make critical comments and who have ongoing interactions with faculty. Other options should be considered, such as eliminating this segment of the portfolio requirement or separating student comments about classes from the portfolio that identifies them by name.

- Sarah submitted her portfolio to the economics faculty, complete with many of her papers from courses during her university career. After the term is over and the portfolios have been graded, Sarah asks to have her portfolio returned. The department chair informs her that they need to keep the portfolios for another year to allow them to do additional analyses.

Analysis: This should be clarified in advance. Students have the right to know what will be done with the data, in this case their own papers. Faculty should let students know how long the portfolios will be kept and should advise students to provide copies if they want to keep original materials.

- You are an assessment consultant and are asked by the department chair to conduct interviews of students for the physical education program. You work with the program chair to develop the interview plan, and once the interviews have been completed, you summarize the results for the department, as agreed. The school dean hears about your report and asks you for a copy.

Analysis: Your negotiated agreement is with the chair, not the dean. Let the chair decide if the dean will receive a copy of the report.

- Your colleagues want to use a standardized exam to assess student competence in the major, but the test costs $50 per student. Your department cannot afford this amount, and faculty decide that they can justify having students pay the price because it will give them useful feedback about their strengths and weaknesses. One of the students objects strenuously to the charge, arguing that she is not interested in taking the test and can't afford to spend the money.

Analysis. Charging students for the test causes harm to them and disproportionately impacts students with limited incomes. Faculty should explore alternative strategies.

- You are on an assessment team that produced a locally developed exam to assess your program. You realize that the exam items vary in difficulty across areas, and the results will undoubtedly show that students are not doing as well in areas that have questions that are written at higher levels of difficulty. Although you have made this point to the committee, no one seems concerned.

Analysis: The principles of competence, fairness, and objectivity apply here. You should not participate in activities that are likely to result in inaccurate conclusions. Perhaps an assessment consultant who can address technical aspects of test design could be asked to assist your team, or perhaps the team should revisit the learning objective to clarify the desired depth of processing.

- Your chair has developed goals and objectives for your program. You realize that your area of expertise is not represented in the goals.

Analysis: This is not directly related to the ethical principles. It is, however, a poor strategic decision to not seek consensus on the learning objectives.

BEFORE YOU BEGIN AN ASSESSMENT PROJECT

You and your colleagues have drafted an assessment plan, and it is time to implement an assessment project. Potential problems can be anticipated and avoided if you pause to reflect on your project before continuing.

Sometimes projects drift from their original focus. For example, the planning committee might select a published test or survey because it is readily available, but forget to consider the alignment of the test with the questions that they want to answer. They should clarify the focus of the project (e.g., directly assessing a learning objective, tracking program characteristics, understanding student perspectives on some issue) and verify that the plans are consistent with that focus. Will the procedures produce data that respond to the questions that are being asked? Will the results lead to an unambiguous interpretation? Imagine various sets of possible results–do they satisfy your purpose?

Consider those who will be affected by the results. Do faculty buy in to the project? Are the issues being assessed high priority for them? Have they been consulted as the project was developed? Are they willing to give serious consideration to the implications of the findings?

Determine who will get the results and how the results will be disseminated. Who will be given access to the raw data? How will you deal with raw data that explicitly name individual employees, students, or courses taught by single individuals? What guarantees can you provide subjects about the confidentiality of their responses, and what mechanisms are in place to preserve this confidentiality? If vulnerable people are involved in the project (e.g., students, untenured faculty), how will you protect the respondents and the messenger if the message is unpopular with recipients?

Data collection can be difficult. How will you gain access to the participants? Will they be contacted in person, online, by telephone, or in classes? Does the process allow you to obtain a representative sample of sufficient size to make meaningful conclusions? Who will conduct the assessment? Are they experienced with the selected methodology? Will they respect ethical guidelines? Will they have the credibility to be effective with the respondents and with the recipients of the report? Can they present the results in an unbiased way?

There should be clear linkages between the focus of the project, the assessment strategy you use, the data analyses, and the decisions about how to use findings. Assessment projects should not be fishing expeditions for something that looks interesting. They should focus on documenting how well students have mastered specific learning objectives or on identifying answers to specific questions.

A pilot study is strongly recommended. It is not unusual for faculty to discover the need to refine procedures or redesign projects based on pilot results. For example, the assignment that faculty thought would produce clear evidence for a program objective may have to be revised to produce effective data for assessment purposes. A pilot study can allow faculty to discover this before committing more resources to the project. Resources are limited, so faculty should use them strategically. It is not unusual for a department to embark on a well-meaning but unsustainable process that becomes a burden to both faculty and students. Avoid this fate by planning your assessment activities carefully, with an eye for what is meaningful, manageable, and sustainable.

5

DIRECT ASSESSMENT TECHNIQUES

Faculty can use a variety of methods to assess student learning. The next three chapters will review many strategies and should provide sufficient information for informed judgements concerning their use. As you read about each potential strategy, think about how you might use it to assess your learning objectives and related program characteristics. Strategies vary in complexity and in demands on student and faculty time. An assessment study may be as simple as including a question on an exam or as complicated as conducting multiple focus groups. As you plan assessment activities, consider practical constraints and select strategies that are realistic, focused, and manageable.

Direct assessments often involve quantitative measurements, and experts have developed a number of techniques for developing measurement procedures and evaluating their quality. Although good assessment can be conducted without expertise in such matters, faculty should be aware that a significant body of work on measurement theory has been developed, and they should seek advice when needed. Most campuses have faculty or staff with expertise in testing and measurement.

PUBLISHED TESTS

An easy response to an assessment mandate is to use already existing, professionally developed tests. Most faculty have taken tests like the

Scholastic Aptitude Test (SAT; http://www.collegeboard.com/) and the American College Test (ACT; http://www.act.org/aap/index.html). These are called *standardized tests* because all students take them under identical conditions.

Many published tests exist, and most campuses have testing officers who have publishers' catalogs and related information. Most published tests were not created as program assessment instruments, so faculty should carefully consider them before using them for that purpose. For example, Graduate Record Examinations (GRE; http://www.gre.org/) were designed for making graduate admissions decisions, and items were created to identify high achievers. Such tests are not particularly sensitive to differences among average or below average students. The GRE General Test measures verbal, quantitative, and analytical skills. The GRE Subject Tests are available for specific disciplines, such as biochemistry, English literature, and psychology.

A variety of other tests for specific programs are available. For example, Major Field Tests were created to assess undergraduate student achievement in a number of disciplines, such as biology, business, chemistry, and history (http://www.ets.org/hea/mft). The Praxis Series tests (http://www.ets.org/praxis/index.html) are designed to assess aspects of teacher competence, and the publisher recommends their use by teacher education programs and state agencies responsible for certifying teachers.

Some standardized tests have been used to assess general education, such as the Academic Profile and Collegiate Assessment of Academic Proficiency (CAAP) tests. The Academic Profile (http://www.ets.org/hea/acpro) was designed to measure "college-level reading, critical thinking, writing, and mathematics in the context of material from the humanities, social sciences, and natural sciences." The CAAP (http://www.act.org/caap/index.html) test is "designed to help institutions measure the academic achievement levels of their students in selected core academic skills" (writing, reading, math, science reasoning, and critical thinking).

Computers have been used to score objective tests for a long time, and publishers are developing and using software that scores essay responses. Such programs are likely to become more common as test publishers reduce their reliance on multiple-choice items and collect more writing samples. Although expensive to develop, these programs allow publishers to provide immediate scores to online test takers and reduce reliance on trained readers. ACCUPLACER (http://www.college-board.com/highered/apr/accu/accu.html) is designed to measure incoming students' competence in reading, writing, and mathematics. This test assesses writing samples with sophisticated software that "knows" when it can generate a score and when it should refer a test to a human for scoring. Research shows that ACCUPLACER's computer-generated scores correlate highly with scores generated by human readers, but sophisticated test takers can generate meaningless answers that can fool the software (Holst & Elliott, 2002). COMPASS e-Write (http://www.act.org/e-write/index.html) is another online writing test that provides electronic scoring of writing samples.

Faculty who are considering the use of a standardized test should review a *specimen set* (copy of the test, test manual, and other materials) and should consider professional reviews of the test, such as those available in the *Mental Measurements Yearbook* (Impara & Plake, 2001). A primary question concerns the alignment of the test with the program objectives and curriculum. Faculty might create an alignment matrix that relates test items or test subscales to their learning objectives, and they should determine if items are current and at the desired depth of processing. Sometimes tests only provide a single score, and this score may be too broad for effective assessment. Practicalities also cannot be ignored. Faculty should consider how much the test costs, if proctors require special training, how much time is needed for testing and scoring, and how they will motivate students to take the test seriously. For example, if they plan to give tests within courses that are scheduled for 50 minutes, they should verify that the test can be administered, completed, and collected in that time; and they should have some confidence that students will be motivated to demonstrate the extent of their learning. Another important consideration is faculty acceptance of the test. If faculty will not act on results, the test will not be useful.

Students are asked to take many tests during their college years, and they have the right to be treated fairly. The American Educational Research Association, the American Psychological Association, and the National Council on Measurement in Education created a Joint Committee on Testing Practices, and in 1994 this committee developed a Code of Fair Testing Practices in Education. This code specifies the obligations of test developers and test users of educational tests, such as tests used for admissions, assessment, diagnosis, and placement. Assessment efforts often make use of data used for other purposes, such as admissions or course grading. This code was not meant to apply to routine classroom exams, but if faculty embed assessment within these exams, they should be aware of its principles. Many of these guidelines are reasonable for any student testing, but much of the concern in the Code is over *high-stakes testing*, such as testing that determines if individual students can be admitted into college or if remedial courses will be required.

The Code specifies that test developers should "strive for fairness" for all test takers. They should avoid content or language that might be offensive to individual test takers, eliminate test items that unfairly discriminate against groups of test takers, ensure that tests are valid, and provide reasonable accommodations to students with special needs. Test publishers are expected to provide information needed to make informed judgments to those who select and use tests. This includes explicit statements of what is being measured, who can be measured fairly, test development procedures, evidence of test effectiveness for recommended uses, limitations affecting test use, specialized skills needed for test administration and scoring, norm group characteristics, information needed to interpret scores accurately, and warnings about possible misuses of test scores. Test publishers are expected to provide specimen sets to professionals who select tests to enable them to make independent judgments concerning the appropriateness of the test for their use.

Published tests, like all assessment strategies, have strengths and limitations. They generally are carefully developed, highly reliable, professionally scored, and nationally normed. They frequently provide a number of norm groups, such as norms for community colleges, liberal arts colleges, and comprehensive universities. Online versions of tests are increasingly available, and some provide immediate scoring. In addition, some publishers allow faculty to supplement tests with their own items, so tests can be adapted to better serve local needs.

The Conference on College Composition and Communication Committee on Assessment (1995) developed a policy statement concerning the assessment of writing skills. They expressed concern about standardized exams, especially those that do not examine writing samples: " . . . *choosing a correct response from a set of possible answers is not composing"* (Assumptions section, ¶ 8). In addition, they warn that reliance on such tests might mislead students into thinking that good writing is accomplished quickly and conforms to stylistic and grammatical rules without concern for meaning. They suggest that funds allocated for writing assessment might be better spent compensating local readers than by purchasing published tests because faculty development and curriculum reform are inevitable when faculty work together to do assessment.

Published tests are not useful as direct measures for program assessment if they do not align with program learning objectives. Most standardized tests rely heavily on multiple-choice items which often focus on specific facts, but program learning objectives more often emphasize higher-level skills. In addition, local curricula may not include coverage of the relevant content. If the test does not reflect the learning objectives that faculty value and the curricula that students experience, results are likely to be discounted and inconsequential.

Student motivation can be a problem. Staff at some campuses tell horror stories about expensive testing programs that yielded problematic data. Students were enticed to take exams by promises of free pizza or t-shirts, and some responded by randomly filling in answer sheets or completing three-hour exams in minutes. Possible solutions include providing scores to individuals so they can understand their relative strengths, offering prizes to students or groups of students with the highest scores, embedding tests in capstone courses, and making a passing score a graduation requirement.

Standardized tests also cost money, and department budgets may be stretched by ongoing reliance on them. If faculty determine that it is important to compare students to national norms, standardized tests are valuable tools, but the marginal gain from annual testing is questionable. Their occasional use to evaluate the impact of curricular change may be more reasonable, especially if faculty have the goal of helping graduates become more competitive on standardized exams. Although some object to "teaching to the test," this criticism is less reasonable if the test measures the program's learning objectives.

LOCALLY DEVELOPED TESTS

Probably the best way to ensure that tests tap program learning objectives is to create them locally. Faculty could create single test items or groups of items that they embed within course exams, or they could create entire tests that are administered to groups of students, such as seniors in capstone courses. Figure 5.1 describes an ongoing project that uses locally developed exams to assess quantitative skills at University of Wisconsin-Madison. This example illustrates how assessment projects can serve multiple functions and can benefit current and future students.

Traditional test items have essay, multiple-choice, true-false, matching, or completion formats. Figure 5.2 summarizes some characteristics of these formats and suggestions for creating good items (Davis, 1993; McKeachie, 1999; Miller & Miller, 1997; Nilson, 1998). A common distinction is between items that require *recognition* and items that require *recall*. Multiple-choice and matching items require recognition of right answers. Completion items and essay questions require recall because test takers must generate the answer on their own. Faculty who create the test should consider if their interest is in assessing recognition, recall, or deeper levels of processing. Another common distinction is between *speed* and *power* tests. Speed tests measure how quickly students can do simple things, and power tests measure deep processing. The goal of testing is to assess how well students have mastered learning objectives. If higher-order thinking skills are being examined, power tests should be used because students will need time to reflect on and compose their answers. Test questions should be phrased in simple, direct language to ensure that students understand what is being asked of them, and tests should align with courses and curricula to guarantee that students have been exposed to appropriate learning opportunities. In addition, test makers should develop tests that have sampling validity; that is, the test items should cover the entire range of interest, rather than isolated segments.

Traditional testing methods have been criticized, especially their reliance on multiple-choice formats. For example, the Association of American Colleges and Universities (2002) warns that "Multiple choice tests, in particular, provide little evidence of the analytical power, creativity, resourcefulness, empathy, and abilities to apply knowledge and

FIGURE 5.1
EMBEDDED ASSESSMENT OF QUANTITATIVE SKILLS

Faculty members in the Quantitative Assessment Committee at the University of Wisconsin-Madison found a useful way to help faculty and students while doing assessment (Robbin & Alvarez-Adem, 2001). Each semester they invite faculty who teach courses that build on a mathematical foundation to identify mathematical or statistical skills essential for successful course completion. Then they create a competency exam based on these identified skills, and faculty administer it early in the semester. Exams are scored by mathematics graduate students, and they provide formative feedback to each student and aggregated results to each faculty member. Many of the involved courses are in the general education program, such as economics, mathematics, and physics courses, but they also provide this service to faculty who teach junior-level major courses that have a quantitative basis, including courses in engineering, nursing, and the social sciences. This is not a small operation. Tests were administered to over 2,000 students in 16 courses during the 2000-2001 academic year.

Results have been enlightening for faculty. For example, they found that nearly half the students in teacher-preparation mathematics courses could not multiply and divide numbers with decimals, and this led to immediate curricular changes. Faculty also have discovered other uses for their tests. For example, food science faculty began with a test created for a required major course, then used it as a pretest for all new students. They provide a follow-up workshop for students with identified problems.

This effort has been sustained since 1990 and continues to grow each year because faculty find it useful. Faculty who teach the basic quantitative methods courses use project results to assess their program, and they have revised courses and refocused their teaching to reduce identified problems. Faculty on the Quantitative Assessment Committee are pleased that faculty outside of the mathematics department are becoming more aware of the mathematical basis for their courses and are examining the validity of their assumptions about students' incoming skills. There has also been increased, fruitful communication between mathematics faculty and faculty in other disciplines on how to develop student mathematical competence.

transfer skills from one environment to another that students will need for college success" (Barriers to Readiness section, ¶ 6), and they remind us that "Learning is more than the acquisition of discrete facts. . . . students need to know facts, but even more importantly how to interpret and what to do with those facts" (Barriers to Readiness section, ¶ 4).

Wiggins (1998) argues that "Conventional test questions, be they from national tests or the teacher down the hall, do not replicate the kinds of challenges that adults face in the workplace, in civic affairs, or

FIGURE 5.2
COMMON TEST ITEM FORMATS

Item Type	Characteristics and Suggestions
Completion	These items require students to fill-in-the-blank with appropriate terms or phrases. They appear to be best for testing vocabulary and basic knowledge, and they avoid giving students credit for guessing by requiring recall, rather than recognition. Scoring can be difficult if more than one answer could be correct. When writing these items, avoid giving cues to correct responses (such as using "a" versus "an" or "was" versus "were" and providing varying amounts of space for answers); create questions with answers that are in the middle or end of the item, rather than at the beginning; and avoid textbook quotes that lack meaning out of context.
Essay	Essay questions are very popular and can be used to assess higher-order thinking skills. They generally ask for explanations and justifications, rather than memorized lists. Key words in essay questions are *summarize, evaluate, contrast, explain, describe, define, compare, discuss, criticize, justify, trace, interpret, prove,* and *illustrate* (Moss & Holder, 1988). Avoid questions that are too broad, for example, "Write everything you know about the Civil War." A format that you might find useful is to assign students a role, a task, and an audience. For example, a question might ask students to be an expert in forensic psychology (the role) who is to appear before a parole board of intelligent laymen (the audience) to explain psychological factors associated with recidivism (the task). Such questions can provide data for the authentic assessment of important learning objectives.
Matching	Usually these questions are presented as two columns, and students are required to associate elements in column B with elements in column A. Such items are easy to score, but they are relatively difficult to construct and they seem best suited for testing knowledge of factual information, rather than deeper levels of understanding. If each answer can be used only once, students can use elimination to select answers without knowing the material. When writing these items, keep the elements in the columns short, list the elements in a logical order (e.g., alphabetical or numerical order), tell students if responses can be used more than once, keep all segments of the question on the same page of the test, and consider including some extra elements in column B to reduce guessing by elimination.

Item Type	Characteristics and Suggestions
Multiple-choice	Multiple-choice questions are popular because they can measure many concepts in a short period of time, and they generally are better than other objective questions at assessing higher-order thinking. They are easy to score, and item banks associated with popular textbooks often are available. Writing good items takes time, and there is strong temptation to emphasize facts, rather than understanding. Multiple-choice items have three parts: the stem, the correct answer, and the incorrect alternatives (distractors). When writing items, create stems that are positively phrased (so double negatives do not confuse test takers), that express a complete thought, that avoid unnecessary detail, and that avoid giving clues (such as using "a" versus "an"). Avoid redundant phrasing in response options by integrating common phrasing into the stem. If response options have a natural order (e.g., from small to large), give them in order so students can easily see the range. Distractors should be designed to attract students who have common misconceptions. They should not be written to "trick" students into selecting the wrong answer.
True-false	True-false items are relatively easy to construct and grade, but they appear to be best at assessing factual knowledge, rather than deep understanding. When writing true-false questions, avoid cues. For example, "usually" and "often" generally suggest true statements, and "always" and "every" generally suggest false statements. Avoid textbook quotes which lack meaning out of context, and avoid response patterns. For example, a true answer should just as likely follow a true item as a false item.

in their personal lives" (p. 22). He argues that faculty should embed more authentic testing in courses to provide ongoing, formative feedback on student progress toward understanding what they are learning. Figure 5.3 contrasts authentic and traditional tests. Wiggins does not argue for the elimination of traditional tests, but he strongly advocates less reliance on them. In addition, he acknowledges that traditional tests may have strong validity if they correlate highly with authentic measures, but they generally lack the formative and motivational benefits of authentic tests.

Authentic-style assessments need not be complicated. For example, faculty at Mary Washington College (2002) assess aspects of information

FIGURE 5.3
AUTHENTIC VERSUS TRADITIONAL TESTS

Authentic Test	Traditional Test
Requires students to create solutions to complex, real-world problems by integrating and applying what they have learned.	More often requires students to recall or recognize correct answers.
Usually involves a single, complex task.	Test usually is composed of items that are unrelated to each other.
Can provide direct evidence of student mastery of complex learning objectives.	Usually provides indirect evidence of student mastery of complex learning objectives.
Scoring requires subjective judgment.	Scoring more often is mechanical.
Variety of answers may be acceptable, although some may be better than others.	Usually there is one correct answer.
Expectations and criteria may be known in advance; e.g., a rubric may be provided to students.	Scoring criteria generally are not known in advance.
Generally, formative feedback is provided to students.	More often summative feedback is provided to students, telling them what they don't know, rather than how to improve.
Opportunities may be available to redo or revise the product.	Usually there is one-chance testing, with no opportunity for revision.
May occur in a complex environment, such as a field placement or laboratory.	Usually done as a timed, paper-and-pencil test in a classroom.
May involve students working cooperatively or with other colleagues to construct a solution.	Usually students take the test by themselves.
May encourage deeper learning.	May encourage memorization and "cramming."

literacy by asking students to respond to email messages and to make prescribed changes in word processor and spreadsheet documents. Class assignments and course activities also provide opportunities to integrate authentic assessment into courses, and these will be described in the next section.

Locally developed tests have a number of strengths. They allow faculty to explicitly tie assessments to program objectives, and appropriate mixes of items allow this to be done efficiently. These tests are likely to be less reliable than published tests, but, if well constructed, they are likely to have good validity. Because local faculty write the test, they should be interested in the results and willing to use them, and the discussion of results should easily lead to reflection on student learning and program support for it.

Norm groups usually are not available for locally developed tests, but faculty from campuses with similar missions could cooperate to develop their own norms, and they could assess student work together or provide independent assessment of each other's student work. This might add to the credibility of findings because unbiased "outsiders" have contributed scoring decisions or benchmarking information. Creating and scoring exams does take time, but if exams are embedded within courses, this is time already included in routine faculty workloads. As with standardized tests, student motivation is important so that students display the extent of their learning.

EMBEDDED ASSIGNMENTS AND COURSE ACTIVITIES

Standardized and locally developed tests generally are given to groups of students simultaneously, frequently with time restrictions, but assessments also can be embedded as in-class activities or homework assignments. For example, embedded assignments and course activities could be integrated into:

- Classroom assessment activities.
- Community service learning and other fieldwork activities.
- Culminating projects, such as senior theses and papers in capstone courses.
- Group projects and presentations.

- Homework assignments.

- In-class presentations.

- In-class writing assignments.

- Poster presentations and student research conferences.

- Senior recitals and exhibitions.

These assignments might provide authentic assessment of important learning objectives, especially if case studies (Honan & Rule, 2002), problem-based learning (Duch, Groh, & Allen, 2001), or other real-world activities are involved. Students taking community service learning or fieldwork classes (Heffernan, 2001) often are required to analyze relationships between their academic learning and what they learn in their placements, directly demonstrating their mastery of relevant learning objectives. In addition, community supervisors could be asked to assess students' abilities to deal effectively with clients, to respect ethical standards, and to communicate professionally; and their involvement should help them make better contributions to the cohesive curriculum because they are aware of its learning objectives.

Assessment projects can be routinely integrated into specific courses, and, like most embedded assessments, they can serve multiple functions. For example, the management program at the Central Missouri State University's Harmon College of Business Administration gives a battery of tests to students in their orientation course and again in their capstone course. Students learn about program objectives early in their academic careers, and they are given individual feedback on their entering skills so they can focus on identified deficiencies (Palomba & Palomba, 2001). This strategy allows faculty to examine both value-added and absolute attainment components of student learning.

Major assignments, such as senior projects or theses, can provide valuable assessment data. Assignments that require oral presentations or group work allow faculty to assess content mastery, and they also provide opportunities to assess communication and interpersonal skills. Some programs routinely have senior recitals or exhibitions, and these provide excellent assessment opportunities. For example, the studio arts program in the University of Colorado at Boulder's Department of Fine Arts (2000) invited two external reviewers to evaluate displays at their annual exhibition of graduating seniors' work, turning this celebratory event into an opportunity to collect assessment data.

It is hard to imagine a college or university program that does not have some learning objectives related to students' written communication skills, and these generally are assessed using locally developed writing assignments. The Conference on College Composition and Communication Committee on Assessment (1995) position statement stresses the need to collect writing samples based on reasonable writing assignments for the students being assessed, to evaluate student papers fairly within their social context, and to recognize that writing is a complex process, so the quality of an individual's writing is expected to vary across writing assignments. Their position statement provides specific recommendations, such as collecting more than one writing sample for each student and providing students sufficient time to draft and edit documents. They argue that faculty should assume responsibility for defining and field testing writing tasks, developing scoring guides and reader training procedures, assessing the documents, and using results to improve curriculum and pedagogy.

Angelo and Cross (1993) describe a variety of classroom assessment techniques, and many could be adapted as embedded assessments. For example, the "one-sentence summary" asks students to briefly summarize an important concept, and this technique could be used to examine students' understanding of major concepts, events, or issues in the discipline. Students might be asked to write a one-sentence summary of the American constitution, the concept of "gravity," or Jungian theory. Another technique, "empty outlines," asks students to complete a partially filled out or blank outline that ties key concepts together, and this could be used to analyze students' overall understanding of the discipline. A "background knowledge probe" or "misperception/preconception check" could be used at the beginning of courses to analyze students' mastery of assumed content and skills, and they could be used again to verify progress. Although created to provide formative assessment for faculty who teach specific courses, such embedded assessments could provide quick program assessment information.

What differentiates embedded assessments from other class activities is that they are designed to collect information on specific program learning objectives. In addition, results are pooled across courses and instructors to indicate program accomplishments, not just the learning of students in specific course sections.

These assignments generally are graded, as usual, by course instructors. Individual faculty probably would vary in the criteria they apply when assigning grades, giving more credit for course-specific learning. Copies of student products generally are collected for later assessment. Sometimes small programs accumulate copies for a year or two before analyzing them to ensure that sufficient numbers of materials are examined. Someone usually removes identifying information for students and faculty, and reviewers analyze the work to assess specific objectives. Faculty generally develop specific scoring criteria targeting the learning objectives so readers focus on assessment, rather than grading. As with locally developed exams, faculty on campuses with similar missions might work together to assess materials and to develop norms.

Walvoord and Anderson (1998) suggest an alternative data collection strategy. Faculty develop a common scheme for assessing elements of embedded assignments, do the assessment as they grade, and pool these assessment data across courses. For example, program faculty could adopt a common scoring rubric for assessing critical thinking or written communication skills. Data could be accumulated and analyzed periodically to assess program objectives and to identify trends or responses to curricular changes.

Embedding assessments within course activities and assignments is good practice. Learning can be assessed using direct measures that are aligned with program objectives, and students generally are motivated to show the extent of their learning. As with locally developed tests, faculty who are involved in creating the assessment process are likely to be interested in the results and willing to use them. These assignments should fit easily into courses that are aligned with relevant program learning objectives, and grades should provide important feedback to students. Faculty discussion of scoring criteria should increase their common understanding of program objectives, and if they jointly review student work, their discussion of results and their implications for change can occur with the evidence immediately in mind and available to them.

COMPETENCE INTERVIEWS

Competence interviews are exams which are orally administered. Interviewers can work alone or in groups, and they can interview single students or groups of students. Unlike written exams, interviews allow faculty to ask follow-up questions to clarify the breadth and extent of students' understanding. Competence interviews can be used to directly assess a number of learning objectives, such as knowledge of key terms, theories, and findings in the discipline; the ability to integrate information to discuss complex problems or issues; and communication, critical thinking, and interpersonal skills.

Competence interviews are common in foreign language programs, especially if the ability to converse in the language is among the program's learning objectives. Student conversational ability is assessed in an authentic process, and faculty are able to evaluate fluency as well as competency of language use, such as appropriate use of vocabulary, grammar, and syntax. Competence interviews also are common in professional programs, such as social work and nursing. Such interviews might simulate interactions with clients, or they may be more traditional in nature, based on a series of questions and answers.

Many of us have experienced competence interviews from the student's perspective—our dissertation defense—and we should remember these experiences when designing competence interviews for our own students. Procedures which are too threatening are likely to frustrate students and keep them from demonstrating the extent of their learning.

Competence interviews can be *structured* or *unstructured*. Structured interviews involve asking the same questions each time, and interviewers follow a well-rehearsed script. When conducting unstructured interviews, interviewers are allowed to vary their questions, and the process is more open. Skilled interviewers can solicit information on deep processing by encouraging students to elaborate on and explain ideas. More information on interviewing skills is provided in the next chapter.

Interviewers generally ask *open-ended questions*, rather than *closed-ended questions*. Open-ended questions invite respondents to generate longer, more thoughtful replies. Closed-ended questions invite respondents to provide brief answers that are likely to be either correct or wrong. "Name the current president of the United States" is a closed-ended question, while "Describe how checks and balances are built into our national government," "How well do these checks and balances work?" and "What evidence leads you to that conclusion?" are open-ended questions.

Faculty should develop clear understanding of the purpose of the interviews, how they will be conducted, and how they will be scored. It is sometimes difficult to conduct interviews while scoring them, and interviewers sometimes work in teams, separating these roles. Faculty also could invite community professionals to participate. Their input could give fresh perspectives on student attainment, program objectives, and the curriculum.

Those who conduct competence interviews generally require training so that collected information can be aggregated meaningfully. Figure 5.4 describes Kansas State University's competence interviews for assessing general education objectives.

Practical issues require attention. Interviews take time to conduct and may be difficult to schedule. Interview protocols (scripts) must be developed and tested. Subjective judgments are used to assess learning, and their reliability and validity can be improved by developing explicit scoring criteria and by carefully training interviewers and raters. As with other procedures, student motivation is important.

Competence interviews are not the most efficient way to get some types of information, such as student knowledge of specific facts. Interviews could be combined with other assessment activities. For example, students could take written exams that assess their knowledge of facts, followed by interviews designed to assess their deeper levels of understanding.

PORTFOLIOS

Portfolios are becoming increasingly popular for course grading and program assessment. Students are required to create compilations of their work, and they usually are required to reflect on their achievement of learning objectives and how the presented evidence supports their conclusions. Portfolio requirements engage students in the assessment process and encourage them to take responsibility for and pride in their learning. Students may develop better understanding of their own academic growth, and they may find their portfolios useful when applying for jobs or graduate programs. School principals in some states routinely expect teaching applicants to bring portfolios to interviews, and portfolios have a long history in other disciplines, such as architecture, art, design, and photography. Here are a few examples of campus portfolio experiences:

FIGURE 5.4
GENERAL EDUCATION COMPETENCE INTERVIEWS

Kansas State University faculty use General Education Senior Interviews to assess general education objectives (IDEA Center, 1998). Faculty participate in a workshop to learn how to establish rapport with students, conduct the interview as a conversation rather than an inquisition, and complete evaluation forms. Teams of three faculty work together during two weeks of interviews, and each interview is scheduled for 45 to 50 minutes, followed by ten to 15 minutes for completing the assessment.

Senior students who began at the university as freshmen are randomly selected from each college, and they receive $25 for participating. Instructions are distributed several weeks before the interview, and they encourage students to spend several hours considering their response to a broad question: "Please discuss a topic that you find personally interesting or important and that is not related to your major. Identify two that you would like to discuss. Although usually there is only time to talk about one topic, you can discuss the second if time allows" (IDEA Center, 1998, p. 8).

Students are allowed to discuss the question with friends and to bring notes with them to the interview. As the interview begins, they are assured that the interviewers are assessing the program, rather than individual students, and that their responses and names will be kept confidential. Faculty follow a structured interview protocol and ask clarifying questions to allow them to assess responses, such as, "I think I understand what you are saying, but could you tell us what your personal viewpoint is about this topic?" (IDEA Center, 1998, p. 21).

Faculty independently rate each student and attempt to reach consensus if there is disagreement. Thirteen rating scales are used for each student, and they assess a variety of dimensions, such as how well students display broad interest in topics outside of their discipline, demonstrate depth of understanding, provide evidence supporting their perspective, discuss alternative perspectives, and use oral communication and critical thinking skills.

- Faculty at Alverno College require students to develop a diagnostic digital portfolio, and it is used developmentally by students and advisors to track student growth and by faculty to improve courses and curricula. Student self-assessment is an important component of this process (Loacker, 2002).

- Faculty at Ferris State University (2002) collect writing portfolios from all campus writing courses, and teams of reviewers rate the attainment of their general education writing objectives. Reviewers also examine the types of writing that students do to ensure a cohesive curriculum.

- Indiana University-Purdue University Indianapolis (IUPUI) pilot tested the use of an electronic portfolio in 2000/2001, and they attempted to develop a model with broad campus support that satisfied concerns about security, privacy, and usefulness for assessment. Each student portfolio is organized into three sections: About Me (students describe their individual backgrounds), My Academic Goals and Plans (students develop plans in the freshman year then refine them as they progress), and Principles of Undergraduate Learning (students present evidence of their attainment of relevant learning objectives, including general education objectives). Preliminary work suggested the need to reassure faculty that portfolios are not to be used to evaluate faculty themselves, and that it is acceptable to share materials that are works-in-progress; and students required help to learn how to reflect on their own learning (Banta & Hamilton, 2002).

- New Century College requires all students to develop portfolios, and a faculty reviewer must approve the portfolio before a student can graduate. Each portfolio must include a self-assessment based on evidence presented for nine campus-wide competencies, a reflective essay, and a career development plan. Faculty evaluate portfolios using a rubric that examines the completeness and quality of the evidence and the self-analysis. Details are provided on their web site (New Century College, 2002).

- Olivet College requires students to build portfolios as they progress through the curriculum. Students must demonstrate satisfaction of lower-division learning goals before they can move into upper-division coursework, and they must demonstrate satisfaction of program goals before they graduate. Freshmen begin structuring their portfolios around general education objectives in a required portfolio course where they learn how to provide evidence and reflect on its meaning, and most majors provide portfolio seminars for their students (Petrulis, 2002). Faculty mentors evaluate all portfolios each semester, providing developmental support for each student (Olivet College, 2002).

Two basic types of portfolios are common: *showcase portfolios* and *developmental portfolios*. Showcase portfolios document the extent of learning by featuring the student's best work. Developmental portfolios are designed to show student progress, and they include evidence of growth by comparing products from early and late stages of the student's academic career. Portfolios also come in different formats. Although traditional paper portfolios in binders or folders are common, some programs require *webfolios* that are submitted on web sites or compact discs (e.g., Sterken, 1999). As students become more proficient in the development of these electronic products, and as faculty become more comfortable accessing them, webfolios will become more popular because they help departments avoid the hassle of storing and distributing printed records.

Faculty must make a number of decisions before portfolios are assigned, and they should answer questions like these:

- What is the purpose of the requirement–to document student learning, to demonstrate student development, to learn about students' reflections on their learning, to create a document useful to students, to help students grow through personal reflection on their personal goals?

- When and how will students be told about the requirement, including what materials they need to collect or to produce for it?

- Will the portfolios be used developmentally or will they be submitted only as students near graduation?

- Will portfolios be showcase or developmental?

- Are there minimum and maximum lengths or sizes for portfolios?

- Who will decide which materials will be included in portfolios–faculty or students?

- What elements will be required in the portfolio–evidence only from courses in the discipline, other types of evidence, evidence directly tied to learning objectives, previously graded products or clean copies?

- Will students be graded on the portfolios? If so, how and by whom?

- How will the portfolios be assessed to evaluate and improve the program?

- What can be done for students who have inadequate evidence through no fault of their own?

- What will motivate students to take the portfolio assignment seriously?

- How will the portfolio be submitted–hard copy or electronic copy?

- Who "owns" the portfolios–students or the program?

- Who has access to the portfolios and for what purposes?

- How will student privacy and confidentiality be protected?

Faculty should have a clear idea of what information will be needed and how that information will be used. If their major intent is to directly assess student mastery of program learning objectives, they probably should ask students to organize their portfolios around these objectives and to reflect on their attainment. If their program objectives call for value-added information or if portfolios will be used for advising, developmental portfolios may be more useful, but if the program objectives emphasize absolute attainment, showcase portfolios probably are better.

Portfolio assignments should clarify faculty expectations for portfolio content, length, organization, and comprehensiveness. Students generally include products from their courses, such as term papers and exams, but they also may be allowed to use other types of evidence, such as documentation from work or volunteer experiences or products created in courses outside the program.

Portfolio assignments can be integrated into the curriculum, and they can be used during advising. For example, instructors could design assignments with portfolios in mind and remind students that these assignments should be saved for their portfolios. Faculty may require some specific assignments in the portfolio, such as capstone course papers or reports completed in research methods classes. Advisors could periodically review draft portfolios with their advisees and discuss their progress, integrating the portfolio into a developmental assessment process. Some departments ask students to analyze long-term goals, such as career goals, in their portfolios. Students could plan their use of elective courses to meet their personal goals, and they may be required to discuss how their education has helped them move toward their attainment. In this way, the assessment process serves multiple functions–student development, as well as assessment.

Faculty also must decide how to encourage students to submit useful portfolios and how to structure the assignments to promote student learning. Most programs require students to submit portfolios as a course or graduation requirement. To encourage students to submit quality portfolios, some programs require students to meet a minimum standard of performance to graduate, while other programs grade portfolios and use that grade as all or part of a class grade. If students are not motivated to prepare quality portfolios, the process probably will not be useful, and students who put a lot of work into their portfolios may be resentful. Pass/fail grading probably is the easiest, but may not motivate students to submit quality portfolios. Some programs grade students on the total portfolio, including the evidence from prior classes, but this approach suffers from the critique of "double grading" prior work. If only the reflective essay is graded, there may be insufficient student motivation to submit a well-documented file. A popular procedure is to grade students on the reflective part of the portfolio and on the completeness of the evidence, but not on the quality of previously graded work.

Faculty should decide how they will handle students who have inadequate evidence for their portfolios. Students may have good reasons for not having appropriate materials. For example, transfer students may have taken classes at institutions that did not encourage them to save their work, and some students may have depended on storage media that failed. It seems reasonable to provide exceptions for such students and to allow them to demonstrate their learning in other ways.

Faculty in small programs may enjoy reading the handful of portfolios submitted each year, but this joy could diminish in larger programs that annually collect rooms full of thick portfolios. Scoring rubrics or other techniques that help faculty review materials efficiently and effectively are crucial to sustaining faculty involvement in portfolio use. Faculty also might consider sampling strategies, such as carefully analyzing a random sample of portfolios or only a few objectives each year or collecting portfolios from some, rather than all, students. For example, some programs annually invite a few representative students to develop portfolios, and these students are awarded stipends or course credit for their effort. Faculty considering the use of portfolios for program assessment should consider student and faculty workload demands, alternative assessment strategies, how portfolios will be analyzed, how portfolio reviewers will be trained, and how projects will be sustained *before* they ask students to generate these products (Lopez, 1998).

Portfolios have a number of strengths. Because evidence generally is from experiences within the program, gaps in the curriculum are easily identified and the discussion of portfolio results focuses faculty on student learning and program support for it. The workload for faculty and students can be high, and preserving student privacy and confidentiality can be a challenge. Students should be aware that faculty will review the portfolios, and this may cause them to be cautious in criticizing the program or their own learning.

COLLECTIVE PORTFOLIOS

Just reading the last section may have discouraged you from considering portfolios, especially if you think it might involve reviewing huge collections of materials for hundreds of students each term. An alternative exists. Rather than ask students to prepare individual portfolios, faculty can create collective portfolios, collections of student work that are created by faculty for assessment purposes.

Faculty decide which objectives are to be examined, identify relevant student materials (e.g., course exams and assignments), decide on a sampling scheme, then collect the materials and assess them. The sampling scheme might involve collecting materials from whole classes, random samples of students within classes, *systematic samples*, or *purposeful samples*. Systematic samples are collected using a systematic process, such as collecting products from every tenth student on a class list. Purposeful samples are created using predetermined criteria. For example, each instructor may select the work of the lowest, middle, and highest 10% of their class. In this way, faculty know that they are not just examining the strongest or weakest students. When interpreting results, faculty should consider how data were collected because the proportion of underachieving students might vary with sampling technique. Here are a few examples of collective portfolio projects:

- Faculty in the University of Colorado at Boulder's Department of Physics (2001) routinely assess lab projects from a junior-level laboratory course and term papers and projects from their senior capstone course. They have found weaknesses in writing style and clarity and have made curricular changes to place more emphasis on the development of these skills.

- Faculty at Mary Washington College (2002) require all baccalaureate students to complete writing intensive courses in their majors. They periodically collect samples of papers in senior-level courses and use scoring rubrics to review learning objectives associated with writing. In their 2002 analysis, they found that nearly 98% of their students are competent writers.

- Johnson County Community College uses an institutional portfolio to assess its general education program. Faculty from multiple disciplines review student work to assess learning objectives associated with mathematics, writing, speaking, culture and ethics, modes of inquiry, and problem solving. Results, based on the application of holistic rubrics, are compiled by the Office of Institutional Research, and faculty review them and act on what they learn (Seybert, 2002).

- Faculty in California State University, Sacramento's Department of Sociology (2000) collected papers from samples of A, B, and C students in core upper-division courses in the major. They examined two learning goals, written communication skills, and the mastery of basic sociological concepts and theories; and they reviewed materials to identify outstanding work, satisfactory work, inadequate work, and ideas to address identified deficiencies. Their analysis led to a number of suggestions for improving writing assignments and a recognition of the need to implement these improvements while respecting individual faculty control over their courses.

Collective portfolios can be analyzed early in the assessment cycle, even before faculty examine curriculum alignment or plan carefully targeted embedded assignments. All that is needed is a group of faculty who are willing to share some of their student products and discuss what these products tell them about student learning. The process has more potential if the course materials are designed to align with specific objectives. For example, if students are not told in an assignment to compare the relative usefulness of alternative theoretical approaches, faculty may be unable to effectively assess this type of objective. The process is likely to evolve as faculty discover limitations of the evidence available for review.

Faculty are so accustomed to grading that special attention is required to keep them focused on assessing objectives. If they are examining student documents to assess writing skills, they probably can make reasonably reliable and valid judgments quickly, without getting bogged down in other aspects of the papers. Scoring rubrics are particularly effective for this purpose.

Like traditional portfolios, collective portfolios can provide useful assessment information, and they impose no additional work on students. Assessment results are likely to have greater reliability and validity if the relevant exam questions and assignments are designed to assess specific learning objectives. Preplanning embedded assessment gives faculty more control of the process, aligns coursework with program learning objectives, and should allow faculty to get more benefit from the use of collective portfolios.

SUMMARY OF DIRECT ASSESSMENT TECHNIQUES

Each of the direct assessment techniques described in this chapter has potential strengths and limitations, as summarized in Figure 5.5. As faculty select and refine assessment strategies, they should design projects that exploit the strengths and minimize the risks associated with the techniques they employ.

FIGURE 5.5

STRENGTHS AND LIMITATIONS OF
DIRECT ASSESSMENT TECNIQUES

Technique	Potential Strengths	Potential Limitations
Published tests	• Can provide direct evidence of student mastery of learning objectives. • They generally are carefully developed, highly reliable, professionally scored, and nationally normed. • They frequently provide a number of norm groups, such as norms for community colleges, liberal arts colleges, and comprehensive universities. • Online versions of tests are increasingly available, and some provide immediate scoring. • Some publishers allow faculty to supplement tests with their own items, so tests can be adapted to better serve local needs.	• If the test does not reflect the learning objectives that faculty value and the curricula that students experience, results are likely to be discounted and inconsequential. • Most published tests rely heavily on multiple-choice items that often focus on specific facts, but program learning objectives more often emphasize higher-level skills. • Test scores may reflect criteria that are too broad for meaningful assessment. • Students may not take the test seriously if test results have no impact on their lives. • Tests can be expensive. • The marginal gain from annual testing may be low. • Faculty may object to standardized exam scores on general principles, leading them to ignore results.
Locally developed tests	• Can provide direct evidence of student mastery of learning objectives. • Appropriate mixes of items allow faculty to address various types of learning objectives. • Can provide for authentic assessment of higher-level learning.	• These exams are likely to be less reliable than published exams. • Reliability and validity generally are unknown. • Creating effective exams requires time and skill. • Scoring exams takes time.

(continued on page 100)

Technique	Potential Strengths	Potential Limitations
	• Students generally are motivated to display the extent of their learning. • If well constructed, they are likely to have good validity. • Because local faculty write the exam, they are likely to be interested in results and willing to use them. • Can be integrated into routine faculty workloads. • Campuses with similar missions could decide to develop their own norms, and they could assess student work together or provide independent assessment of each other's student work. • Discussion of results focuses faculty on student learning and program support for it.	• Traditional testing methods may not provide authentic measurement. • Norms generally are not available.
Embedded assignments and course activities	• Can provide direct evidence of student mastery of learning objectives. • Out-of-class assignments are not restricted to time constraints typical for exams. • Students are generally motivated to demonstrate the extent of their learning. • Can provide authentic assessment of learning objectives. • Can involve ratings by fieldwork supervisors. • Can provide a context for assessing communication and teamwork skills, as well as other types of learning objectives.	• Requires time to develop and coordinate. • Requires faculty trust that the program will be assessed, not individual teachers. • Reliability and validity generally are unknown. • Norms generally are not available.

Technique	Potential Strengths	Potential Limitations
	• Can be used for grading as well as assessment. • Faculty who develop the procedures are likely to be interested in results and willing to use them. • Discussion of results focuses faculty on student learning and program support for it. • Data collection is unobtrusive to students.	
Competence interviews	• Can provide direct evidence of student mastery of learning objectives. • The interview format allows faculty to probe for the breadth and extent of student learning. • Can be combined with other techniques that more effectively assess knowledge of facts and terms. • Can involve authentic assessment, such as simulated interactions with clients. • Can provide for direct assessment of some student skills, such as oral communication, critical thinking, and problem-solving skills.	• Requires time to develop, coordinate, schedule, and implement. • Interview protocols must be carefully developed. • Subjective judgments must be guided by agreed-upon criteria. • Interviewer training takes time. • Interviewing using unstructured interviews requires expertise. • Not an efficient way to assess knowledge of specific facts and terms. • Some students may be intimidated by the process, reducing their ability to demonstrate their learning.
Portfolios	• Can provide direct evidence of student mastery of learning objectives. • Students are encouraged to take responsibility for and pride in their learning.	• Requires faculty time to prepare the portfolio assignment and to assist students in preparing portfolios. • Requires faculty analysis and, if graded, faculty time to assign grades.

(continued on page 102)

Technique	Potential Strengths	Potential Limitations
	• Students may become more aware of their own academic growth. • Can be used for developmental assessment and can be integrated into the advising process to individualize student planning. • Can help faculty identify curriculum gaps. • Students can use portfolios and the portfolio process to prepare for graduate school or career applications. • Discussion of results focuses faculty on student learning and program support for it. • Webfolios or CD-ROMs can be easily viewed, duplicated, and stored.	• May be difficult to motivate students to take the task seriously. • May be more difficult for transfer students to assemble the portfolio if they haven't saved relevant materials. • Students may refrain from criticizing the program if their portfolio is graded or if their names will be associated with portfolios during the review. • It may be difficult to protect student confidentiality and privacy.
Collective portfolios	• Can provide direct evidence of student mastery of learning objectives. • Students generally are motivated to display the extent of their learning. • Workload demands generally are more manageable than traditional portfolios. • Students are not required to do extra work. • Discussion of results focuses faculty on student learning and program support for it. • Data collection is unobtrusive to students.	• If assignments are not aligned with the objectives being examined, evidence may be problematic. • If sampling is not done well, results may not generalize to the entire program. • Reviewing the materials takes time and planning.

6

INDIRECT ASSESSMENT TECHNIQUES

The preceding chapter reviewed methods that directly assess student learning. Direct techniques require that students display the extent of their learning by doing something, such as responding to a test question or completing a homework assignment. In contrast, indirect techniques involve a report *about* learning rather than a direct demonstration *of* learning. Although most of us would prefer to have students show us rather than tell us about their learning, indirect measures often allow us to obtain information quickly and efficiently. For example, it might take only a few minutes for students to report how well they have mastered our learning objectives, but if they were asked to show this learning, much more time and effort would be required.

Indirect techniques also make unique contributions to program assessment because they allow us to pursue issues in depth and to solicit advice from important stakeholders. For example, faculty might learn that students are not mastering an important learning objective, but they may not know how to respond. They could use an indirect technique, such as interviews or focus groups, to explore this problem and develop an informed response.

Just as with direct techniques, results based on indirect techniques should be reliable and valid. Because what people say they know does not always correspond to what they do know, validity is of particular concern when we indirectly assess our objectives. One way to increase our confidence in the validity of our findings is to compare them to other sources of information. For example, our confidence would be reduced if students report that they are highly skilled in writing, yet direct evidence suggests that their writing is weak. Although we would conclude that these student perceptions are inaccurate, this finding may be important. Opinions, regardless of their accuracy, guide decision-making. Providing optional tutoring in writing may be an ineffective response if students do not recognize their need for such assistance.

Surveys

Surveys elicit information about people's beliefs, experiences, or attitudes. Traditional program reviews relied heavily on surveys, but surveys now share the spotlight with a variety of other techniques. Here are a few examples of assessment studies that used surveys:

- The University of Arizona General Education Assessment Subcommittee used three open-ended questions to survey faculty about the general education (GE) program (University of Arizona, 2000). Questions asked for faculty comments about the GE goals, how the program could be improved, and the GE program's progress to date. Comments were summarized for each question and were categorized as "positive," "mixed," or "negative."

- Staff at California State University, Bakersfield conducted a survey to examine student reactions to their computer labs and email system (Noel, 2002). They emailed students to request their participation and provided a link to an online survey. Results included useful suggestions on how to improve the labs (e.g., changing hours of operation and providing better "how-to" assistance) and email system (e.g., making it easier for students to delete unwanted messages).

- Over 2,000 graduating seniors at George Mason University completed an exit survey that assessed their views on their educational experiences and future plans (George Mason University, 2001). Results were summarized for the entire university, each college, and each major.

- Faculty in the University of Illinois at Urbana-Champaign's Department of Electrical and Computer Engineering (2000) asked three groups to assess student learning. Graduating seniors and alumni rated their level of achievement, and faculty rated the "amount of attention" needed for each of their 14 learning objectives. All groups also responded to open-ended questions about their views of the educational process. The online report provides extensive summaries of the findings.

- The University of North Carolina used surveys to assess student learning and various program characteristics (University of North Carolina, 1998). Questions were given to sophomores, seniors, and alumni on a variety of topics, such as instructional quality, personal growth, and academic support services. Results for departments and for the university as a whole are posted online.

Survey questions can be closed-ended or open-ended, and assessment surveys commonly use both formats. *Closed-ended* questions generally require a short response or an answer chosen from a list. *Open-ended* questions allow respondents to create their own answers within broad parameters set by the survey, and they allow faculty to uncover unanticipated results that would have been missed if only closed-ended questions were used. Occasionally closed-ended questions offer a dichotomous choice, such as "agree" versus "disagree" or "used" versus "did not use," but frequently questions provide a range of response options. For example, a *Likert scale* allows respondents to indicate their degree of agreement, with options usually ranging from "Strongly Disagree" to "Strongly Agree." The number of response categories depends on the extent to which respondents can make meaningful differentiations and the importance of reporting results with response gradations. Figure 6.1 provides examples of item formats and items that could be used for program assessment.

Surveys should be carefully designed. One common mistake is to include every question that anyone suggests, creating a hodgepodge of questions that are unrelated to project objectives. Faculty should create short, focused surveys that deliberately address specific issues, and each item should serve a purpose. Surveys generally end with a set of questions that identify respondent characteristics (e.g., age, gender), allowing faculty to describe the sample and to conduct subgroup analyses, such as comparing the responses of younger and older respondents. Faculty who create surveys should avoid questions that are ambiguous, biased, or

Figure 6.1
Common Survey Formats

Type of Item	Example
Checklist	Please indicate which of the activities you feel competent to perform. __ Develop an investment plan. __ Interpret a financial report. __ Provide feedback about an employee's performance. __ Write a case study.
Classification	Organization of the paper: _____ Confusing, unclear _____ Generally clear, minor points of confusion _____ Clear, logical, easy to follow
Frequency	In a typical term, I used the department's computer lab: Never Seldom Sometimes Often
Importance	How important is it for the department to provide career counseling? Unimportant Slightly Important Moderately Important Very Important Extremely Important
Likelihood	How likely are you to apply to a graduate program in the next five years? Very Unlikely Slightly Unlikely Uncertain Slightly Likely Very Likely
Linear rating scale	Ability to compose paragraphs in standard written English. Unsatisfactory __ | __ | __ | __ | __ | __ | __ Excellent
Likert scale	I am able to write a research paper using MLA standards. Strongly Disagree Disagree Neutral Agree Strongly Agree
Open-ended	Please describe the most important concepts you learned in the program.

Type of Item	Example
Partially closed-ended	Please check the most important factor that led you to major in engineering. ___ Experience in a specific course ___ Experience with a specific instructor ___ Work experience in this or a related field ___ Advice from a career planning office or consultant ___ Advice from family or friends ___ Other: please explain
Quality	Please indicate the quality of instruction in the general education program. Very Poor Poor Good Very Good
Quantitative judgment	Compared to other interns I have supervised, this student's knowledge of the theory and principles of clinical practice is: 1 2 3 4 5 6 7 8 9 10 below average average above average
Ranking	Please indicate your ranking of the importance of the following student learning objectives by assigning ranks from "1" to "4," where "1" is most important and "4" is least important. ___ Computing ___ Critical thinking ___ Speaking ___ Writing

confusing. Allen (1995) offers these suggestions for writing effective survey questions:

- Avoid compound items. (*Did you like the courses and instructors? What about people who like the courses but not the instructors, or vice versa?*)

- For closed-ended questions, be sure to include all possible response categories. (This may require the use of an "Other" category.)

- Avoid vague questions. (*Did you learn because of your efforts or the efforts of the instructor?*)

- Avoid confusing wording. (*I rarely use the library. True__ False__.* Does a "False" answer mean that the person never, often, or always uses the library?)

- Sometimes you have to allow respondents to not answer questions. (*How often do you use your home computer to access online course materials?* How should students without a home computer respond?)

- Avoid wording that might bias responses. (*We expect students to study at least three hours outside of class for each hour in class—please estimate the number of hours you study outside of class for each hour in class.*)

- Avoid questions that threaten or alienate your respondents. (*How concerned are you that our efforts to increase campus diversity threaten academic quality?*)

- Be careful of order effects, when the response to one question influences the response to a later question. (*Have you ever plagiarized a source when preparing a paper or assignment?* followed by *To what extent have you followed departmental ethical guidelines while completing your degree?*)

- Consider specifying a timeframe. (*How many books have you read in the past six months that were not required for a class?*)

- Avoid negative wording. (*I received ineffective career advice. True__ False__.* Some respondents become confused about what their answers mean.)

- Remember cultural differences. (*If you had a personal problem while a student here, did you use the counseling center or did you consult a professional, such as a priest or therapist?* What about a rabbi, minister, parson, elder, mullah, or other representative of a religion?)

Faculty could survey various stakeholders, and Figure 6.2 suggests possible questions for different target groups. Although the questions are presented in an open-ended format, most could be translated into closed-ended questions. For example, instead of asking "What factors influenced your decision to major in this program?" you could ask "Which of the following factors influenced your decision to major in this program?" followed by a list of options.

FIGURE 6.2
POSSIBLE SURVEY QUESTIONS FOR
DIFFERENT GROUPS OF STAKEHOLDERS

Respondents	Examples
Entering students	• What factors influenced your decision to major in this program? • What do you expect to do with a degree in this area?
Current students	• How could we improve the advising in our program? • What could the department do to help you achieve the program's learning objectives? • How could we improve the tutoring center to better meet your needs?
Exiting students	• How effective was the major in preparing you for a career or for graduate school? • What were the strongest aspects of the major? The weakest? • Which of the department's learning objectives do you believe you have achieved? Which, if any, have you not achieved? What improvements could the department make to help students achieve the objectives?
Alumni	• Are you employed in the area of your major? • How effectively did the program prepare you for your current position? • Which of the department's learning objectives have been especially useful in your career? How well did you master them?
Employers	• Do graduates from our program have the skills and other characteristics necessary to work effectively in your organization? • What are the most important things for students to learn to become effective employees in your organization?

(continued on page 110)

Respondents	Examples
	• In the next five years, in what ways should our program change to better prepare our graduates for positions in your organization?
Program faculty	• What are the most important curricular changes for the department to make in the next five years? • Which of the department's learning objectives are most important? Least important? • Should any of the department's learning objectives be modified or deleted? Should any learning objectives be added to the program? Explain.

A variety of published surveys are available. Figure 6.3 describes the effective use of a published survey in general education courses at Portland State University. Such surveys can provide useful information about program support for student learning. For example, the National Survey of Student Engagement (NSSE; www.iub.edu/~nsse) collects information about undergraduate learning experiences and provides norms on student participation in activities known to enhance learning, such as active and collaborative learning. These norms are used as *benchmarks*, that is, criteria for assessing campus results compared to nationally-developed standards. For example, see Belchier (2000) for a report on NSSE findings at Boise State University. The Higher Education Research Institute (HERI) has collected college freshmen data for over three decades in the Cooperative Institutional Research Program (CIRP; http://www.gseis.ucla.edu/heri/heri.html) and has accumulated results from over 1,700 colleges and universities. HERI provides national norms for many variables of interest to campus planners, such as freshmen career interests and prior experiences with computers. Many campuses routinely use these surveys, but results are not always disseminated to faculty and other campus professionals. Potentially useful data which are not shared are unlikely to improve campus operations.

Faculty who conduct surveys should be careful to obtain reasonable samples. Most survey researchers consider the *response rate*, that is, the proportion of contacted individuals who complete the survey. Results can be biased when the response rate is low. For example, perhaps only

FIGURE 6.3
EFFECTIVE USE OF THE COLLEGE
CLASSROOM ENVIRONMENT SCALE

Portland State University faculty began using the College Classroom Environment Scale (CCES; Winston, et al., 1994) in 1994 (Jessen & Patton, 2002). This survey was developed to assess students' perspectives about the degree of "community" in specific classes, and it has six scales: Cathectic Learning Climate (high student engagement), Professorial Concern (faculty respect and empathy for students), Academic Rigor (academic challenge), Affiliation (mutual peer support), Structure (unambiguous alignment of course activities and grading criteria), and Inimical Ambiance (course atmosphere of hostility, rigidity, and competitiveness).

The general education program for most Portland State students is based on learning communities and an interdisciplinary curriculum, making the CCES scales particularly relevant to their mission. The program begins with a year-long interdisciplinary Freshman Inquiry course, and one of its major goals is to build a learning community among involved students. The CCES is administered annually in all sections of Freshman Inquiry.

Faculty who staff these courses receive reports on their results with normative data based on annual summaries of their courses and aggregated data collected in all Freshman Inquiry courses since 1995. This allows faculty to track feedback for their courses and to compare their courses to other sections.

Jessen and Patton (2002) report lessons they have learned over the years. Students are more likely to take the survey seriously if the faculty member or proctor supports its use and explains the reason for the survey and how data will be used. Data collectors should maintain a professional administrative environment by asking students to not talk during its administration and to share honest, thoughtful, and personal perspectives. Students report appreciating the opportunity to discuss results with their instructors, perhaps because this shows respect for their opinions and leads to changes that improve their educational experience. Faculty also found that responses can vary considerably across sections of classes, even when taught by the same individuals, presumably because of differences in student personalities and learning styles, and this has led to productive discussion of pedagogy with faculty development professionals.

In addition to providing formative feedback to individual faculty, program administrators combine CCES results with other assessment data from course evaluations and portfolio reviews. They use results to focus faculty development initiatives and individual consultations, they invite faculty with consistently positive results to share ideas with colleagues at faculty retreats, and they provide individual support to faculty who receive unusually low ratings. Faculty are encouraged to use CCES results to improve community-building in their courses, to assess the impact of changes in pedagogy, and to document teaching effectiveness during personnel reviews. Overall, CCES scores have exhibited positive trends at Portland State, and because these scores reflect an important component of their mission, they are proud of this accomplishment.

respondents with strong opinions or with negative perspectives return the survey. This concern is reduced if respondents appear to be typical of those who were contacted, and faculty could check to see if respondents' *demographic characteristics* (e.g., gender, age, ethnicity, class level, grades) match the population from which they were drawn. It is more important to obtain *representative* (unbiased) samples than large samples, but reasonably large samples are desired to ensure that the full range of opinions have been observed.

Several strategies may improve response rates. Potential participants should be convinced that their responses will be carefully considered and that ethical procedures are in place to protect their confidentiality. They are more likely to return short, professional-looking surveys than long, amateurish ones. Personal contacts with potential respondents can be helpful. For example, data collectors could collect survey data in classes, or they could hand deliver the surveys and arrange a convenient time for picking them up. Sometimes a reminder helps. Researchers who mail surveys frequently follow-up by mailing reminder postcards or second copies of the surveys to nonrespondents.

Online surveys are becoming increasingly popular (e.g., Noel, 2002). They provide quick, inexpensive access to respondents and automatic, reliable data recording. Faculty must find ways to invite possible respondents to complete the survey and motivate them to complete it, and this could be done in classes, newsletters, email messages, or postcards. Commercial software for constructing online surveys is available, and faculty also might make use of course management systems, such as WebCT or Blackboard. As with all surveys, faculty should be concerned about the representativeness of the sample, and there is a risk that such surveys will be biased in favor of those who have easy Internet access.

Surveys have served an important role in the review of academic programs for years, and they continue to be useful tools. They usually are the least expensive way to obtain feedback from large samples, they can easily collect information on many issues, they can be mailed to distant respondents, and results generally are straightforward to interpret. The analysis of open-ended questions can be difficult, but usually is manageable because answers tend to be short and focused. If surveys are periodically repeated, data can be tracked across time to assess the impact of program changes.

INTERVIEWS

As described in Chapter 5, faculty can conduct competence interviews to directly assess student learning. Traditional interviews also have a place in program assessment. Faculty can use them to indirectly assess student learning and to collect feedback on program characteristics. Interviews involve a conversation, or questions and answers, between interviewers and interviewees, and they provide a sense of immediacy and personal attention that often is lacking with surveys. Here are some assessment studies that used interviews:

- Boise State University freshmen were interviewed weekly to determine their reactions to the college experience (Boise State University, 2002). Interview information was combined with data from weekly journals and a year-end group meeting.

- Harvard University faculty and administrators conducted in-depth, open-ended interviews with approximately 1,600 Harvard seniors over a ten-year period (Light, 2001). Among other findings, Light concluded that students tended to be more productive studying in pairs than alone, that time management is one of the most important skills for students to learn, that significant learning occurs during supervised projects and internships, and that experiences with students of different backgrounds is a significant learning experience. This is an excellent example of a long-term unstructured interview study that led to rich findings about students' educational experiences.

- Seniors at the University of Hawaii, Manoa were interviewed about their experiences in writing intensive classes (Hilgers, Bayer, Stitt-Bergh, & Taniguchi, 1995). Student interviewers were guided by a set of 36 interview questions, and they used a semi-structured approach that allowed some interview flexibility to enhance the conversational flow. An extensive discussion of the methodology and results are included in the article.

- The University of Wisconsin-Oshkosh's Department of English (n.d.) uses a brief exit interview, conducted during the student's last term by the student's advisor and a member of the assessment committee. Students are asked their views about the major, the campus, extracurricular activities, and opportunities for their personal development. The advisor sets up and conducts most of the interview, and an assessment committee member takes notes.

- Truman State University conducts yearly interviews with randomly selected students from either the freshman or junior class (Truman State University, 2002). Topics vary each year, but are focused on curricular and co-curricular issues of interest to the university. The 30-minute interviews are standardized and consist primarily of open-ended questions. Interviewer teams consist of one faculty or administration representative and one student member. Results of the surveys are summarized and posted online.

Although interviews are similar to surveys, their distinguishing characteristic is the opportunity for interaction between interviewer and interviewee, which is both a potential strength and limitation. For example, if a respondent does not understand the meaning of a question, the interviewer can clarify any misunderstanding; however, the interviewer also can decrease the objectivity of the process by providing too much interpretation, by doing so inconsistently, or by inadvertently rewarding respondents for giving the desired or expected response. Faculty might not be the best people to interview students because their dual relationship might keep students from expressing criticism, and faculty might find it difficult to avoid biasing results in other ways. Neutral interviewers generally are preferred.

Structured interviews usually are used for program assessment because they provide consistent data across different interviewers and respondents. They are easier to administer than unstructured interviews, and students can be trained to conduct them. Unstructured interviews (e.g., Light, 2001) can produce rich, in-depth understanding of issues; however, they have questionable reliability and validity unless done by skilled interviewers, and they require considerable time for analysis, limiting their usefulness for most assessment projects.

Interview questions can be closed-ended or open-ended. Common closed-ended questions are dichotomous (e.g., "yes" or "no"), request ratings of magnitude (e.g., "How satisfied are you with your program?"), or include checklists (e.g., "Which of the following factors were most important for your educational success?"). Responses to closed-ended questions are relatively easy to record and analyze. In contrast, open-ended questions provide few restrictions to the interviewee, so recording and analyzing the data are more difficult. Despite this concern, open-ended questions are often used because they can uncover unanticipated results.

Interviews can be conducted one-on-one or in small groups (see the focus group discussion in the next section), and they can be conducted face-to-face, by telephone, or by any other method that provides the opportunity for interaction between interviewer and interviewee. Much of the advice for writing good survey questions also applies to creating interview questions. Here are suggestions for constructing the interview script:

- Begin the interview with straightforward questions to help respondents feel comfortable.

- Be clear about what you want to learn from the interviews and match the questions to these objectives. For example, if you want feedback on improving student learning, you might ask, *What is one thing that the department could do to help you learn more effectively?*

- Encourage respondents to talk about their own experiences and perspectives rather than abstract concepts. For example, *What would help you better prepare for a career?* rather than *What are the most important things that the department should cover in a "careers" course?*

- Provide structure to guide the respondents' answers. Instead of *What do you think about the program?* consider *How could the program be improved to help you prepare for graduate school?*

- Avoid closed-ended questions disguised as open-ended ones. For example, *Did you benefit from your advising sessions?* only requires a yes/no response. Instead, ask *Describe one of the most important benefits of your advising sessions.*

- Give the respondents an opportunity to discuss their most important issues or concerns. You may not have asked the most important questions, so include an all-purpose question at the end. For example, you could end the interview with *Is there anything you would like to tell us about the program that we haven't asked about?*

- Pilot test your script with a small sample. You may discover that some of the questions are difficult to understand, that rephrasing is necessary, or that the flow of questions is difficult to follow. Questions that appeared to be appropriate when viewed in print may not be acceptable when spoken by an interviewer. Pilot testing also provides the opportunity to verify that the procedures, including data recording, are workable.

Because of the opportunity for the interviewer to influence the process, it is essential that interviewers be trained. Conducting mock interview sessions can help identify problems before actual interviews begin. For example, interviewers might introduce bias into the process if they are not aware of subtle aspects of their interpersonal dynamics. Practice sessions also allow interviewers to rehearse the process so that they can be relaxed and fluent when they conduct the actual interviews. Here are some tips for effective interviewing:

- Conduct the interview in an environment that allows the interaction to be confidential and uninterrupted.

- Demonstrate respect for the respondents as *participants* in the assessment process rather than as *subjects*. Explain the purpose of the project, how the data will be used, how the respondent's anonymity or confidentiality will be maintained, and the respondents' rights as participants. Ask if they have any questions.

- Put the respondents at ease. Do more listening than talking. Allow respondents to finish their statements without interruption.

- Match follow-up questions to the project's objectives. For example, if the objective is to obtain student feedback about student advising, don't spend time pursuing other topics.

- Do *not* argue with the respondent's point of view, even if you are convinced that the viewpoint is incorrect. Your role is to obtain the respondents' opinions, not to convert them to your perspective.

- Allow respondents time to process the question. They may not have thought about the issue before, and they may require time to develop a thoughtful response.

- Paraphrase to verify that you have understood the respondent's comments. Respondents will sometimes realize that what they said isn't what they meant, or you may have misunderstood them. Paraphrasing provides an opportunity to improve the accuracy of the data.

- Make sure you know how to record the data and include a backup system. You may be using a tape recorder–if so, consider supplementing the tape with written notes in case the recorder fails or the tape is faulty. Always build in a system for verifying that the tape is functioning or that other data recording procedures are working. Don't forget your pencil and paper!

Obtaining a representative sample is an important challenge. In contrast to surveys, interviews require interpersonal contact, and this can be difficult to arrange. Students who fail to show up for appointments can be a continuing source of frustration to interviewers who are working under tight schedules. One strategy is to pay students for their participation, but even this may not assure widespread participation. Students with exams, families, and jobs may decide at the last minute that showing up for the interview is not worth the small stipends usually available for this purpose. Interviewers might try to catch students in public places, such as the cafeteria or library. Interviews also might be administered in conjunction with other activities, such as advising sessions or club meetings. Interviews with faculty, staff, or alumni can be easier to arrange because it is possible to meet them at their offices or professional sites. Faculty should determine an effective way to secure respondents before investing time and effort in this process.

Phone interviews allow interviewers to reach distant respondents, but connecting with people rather than answering machines can be challenging. Phone interviewers frequently enter responses directly into a computer, and the script can be displayed on the screen as they work. This method of data collection has been hampered by the proliferation of commercially-sponsored "surveys" that are veiled sales pitches, and potential respondents may screen out calls from unknown sources or be suspicious when approached. People have learned that it's easy to hang up, so phone surveys should be short, focused, friendly, and professional. For example, Project Pulse (University of Massachusetts, 2002) has been in place at the University of Massachusetts since 1996, and they routinely administer short, targeted phone surveys on issues of current interest, such as gender equity and class size. Some have reported success using an 800 number. They leave a quick phone message on answering machines and invite potential respondents to call back during hours that the phone will be staffed. If addresses are known, this phone number and invitation also could be distributed via email messages or postcards.

Analyzing interview data requires a thoughtful review of what respondents said, and the summary should be succinct, but with sufficient detail to be useful. The report should be organized to respond to project objectives. For example, if the objective was to understand student views about research experiences in the program, the review could summarize positive experiences, negative experiences, and suggestions for improvement. Results that do not fit a pre-defined objective can be included in an "Other" category that summarizes interesting, but unanticipated findings. Chapter 7 contains more information on analyzing responses to open-ended questions.

Interviews are versatile techniques for obtaining feedback from respondents, and they allow interviewers to query for information and clarify questions. They can, however, be expensive and time-consuming.

FOCUS GROUPS

Focus groups are planned discussions among small groups of participants who are asked a series of carefully constructed questions about their beliefs, attitudes, and experiences. Like interviews, they provide personal interaction as data are collected and allow for probing questions and clarifications. In addition, group members can hear and respond to each other's opinions, and facilitators can uncover the degree of consensus on ideas that emerge during the discussion. Students and others generally enjoy participating in focus groups, especially if they believe their opinions will be respected by the faculty who review the report. Properly conducted focus group can provide in-depth, useful feedback about programs, as illustrated by these examples:

- Staff at California State University, Bakersfield used focus groups to examine their instructional television (ITV) program, and they conducted groups at the main campus and at a satellite campus

(Program Assessment Consultation Team, 2001). Results led to a number of improvements, such as offering a hands-on workshop to new ITV instructors, distributing an ITV frequently-asked-questions sheet to students, hiring student assistants to handle the technical aspects of the classroom, and improving communication links with distant students.

- Students at the California Maritime Academy participated in focus groups to determine their experiences in the general education program and their suggestions for improvement (Paine-Clemes, 2001). Students highlighted the need for hands-on activities, visual aids, positive instructor attitudes, and relevance to their personal goals.

- Staff at Georgetown University's Medical Center (2001) conducted a focus group of first-year medical students to assess student reactions to the orientation session. Results provided a number of suggestions for improving the session. The online report includes an executive summary, the facilitator's questions, and a transcript of student responses.

Effective focus group facilitation requires special skills. Although it often looks easy to an observer, conducting focus groups requires an understanding of group dynamics and the ability to mentally juggle content and process. Facilitators must be able to establish rapport with participants and generate their trust; and they must manage the discussion to engage all participants, elicit the full range of opinions, and keep the process focused on project goals. Credibility is essential for eliciting open, honest participation. Students might be intimidated if facilitators are instructors who could identify them and who hold significant power over them; and most faculty would find it difficult to hear complaints without becoming defensive. Neutral focus group leaders who are not program stakeholders are recommended. Most campuses have faculty who are experienced in qualitative research techniques, including focus groups, such as faculty in psychology, sociology, anthropology, business, nursing, and education. Faculty who want to include focus groups in their program evaluation plans should collaborate with colleagues who have focus group experience.

The facilitator conducts the focus group using a series of prepared questions. The session has three major phases. *Opening questions* in the *warm-up* phase involve everyone in the discussion and make them comfortable with the process; *issue questions* elicit information about the primary objectives of the project; and *closing questions* allow participants to clarify earlier comments and discuss topics not previously addressed, and they bring closure to the process. Examples of focus group questions are presented in Figure 6.4.

Focus groups can be implemented in a variety of ways, ranging from an unstructured, open-ended process to one that is highly structured (McMillin & Noel, 2001). Fewer skills are required to conduct highly structured group interviews, and more skills are required to conduct less-structured, traditional focus groups.

Traditional focus groups are free-flowing discussions among participants, guided by a skilled facilitator who subtly directs the discussion in accordance with predetermined objectives (Morgan & Krueger, 1998). This process leads to in-depth responses to questions, generally with full participation from all group members. The facilitator departs from the script to follow promising leads that arise during the interaction. The data are extensive transcripts of complicated group interactions, and the researcher must invest considerable time to interpret the transcription and write reports.

Structured group interviews are less interactive than traditional focus groups and can be facilitated by people with less training in group dynamics and traditional focus group methodology. The group interview is highly structured, and the report generally provides a few core findings rather than an in-depth analysis. This model is most often used for the formative assessment of specific courses, and standardized procedures have been suggested, such as the Small-Group Instructional Diagnosis (SGID; Bennett, 1987) and the Group Instructional Feedback Technique (GIFT; Angelo & Cross, 1993). Facilitators often are faculty development professionals, and they conduct these interviews in intact classes while the instructor is away. They generally ask three questions that invite students to identify what the instructor is doing well, what the instructor is not doing well, and what specific suggestions might improve the instructor's effectiveness.

	FIGURE 6.4
	FOCUS GROUP SAMPLE QUESTIONS
Purpose of Question	**Examples**
Warm-up	• I'd like everyone to start out by stating a word or phrase that best describes your view of the program.
Issue 1: Career preparation	• Please tell us what career you are interested in pursuing after graduation. • How has the program helped you prepare for your career or future activities?
Issue 2: Advising	• We are interested in your advising experiences in the program. Could you tell us about your first advising experience in the department? • What did you find most useful in your interactions with your advisor? • What would you like our advisors to do differently?
Issue 3: Curriculum	• Thinking about the curriculum and the required courses, how well do you think they prepared you for upper-division work? • What should be changed about the curriculum to better prepare you for your career or for graduate school?
Closing	• We've covered a lot of ground today, but we know you might still have other input about the program. Is there anything you would like to say about the program that hasn't been discussed already?

Millis (1999, 2001) and colleagues at the United States Air Force Academy conduct SGIDs and have augmented them with a brief survey and small-group exercise. The facilitator begins by giving each participant an index card and asking them to rate the quality of the course using a 5-point scale and to provide a word or phrase that describes their reaction to it. Students share what they have written with the group, followed by a discussion of the focus group questions. Then the facilitator asks participants to form smaller groups (roundtables) that create two lists (the most positive aspects of the course and things that should be improved), and the small groups are asked to consensually rank order the top few items on each list. A report is provided to the instructor that summarizes the index card results in a histogram (see a simulated example in Figure 6.5), provides a transcript of the large-group interview, and presents the roundtable rank-ordered lists in a table. The entire process produces a quick turnaround of information, provides quantitative and qualitative results, and has proven to be useful for course improvement.

Noel (2001b) and his colleagues conduct program assessment focus groups that combine characteristics of traditional focus groups and the Air Force Academy group interviews. They use the index card and roundtable exercises, and they add a short questionnaire that collects demographic information and data on students' long-term goals. In addition, they survey students at the end of the session to collect feedback on the conduct of the group and to determine how well it allowed participants to freely contribute their ideas. Assessment center staff work with department chairs to identify the issues to be discussed, and assessment center student assistants conduct these modified focus groups using about an hour of class time. Facilitators probe for additional information during the whole-group discussion and encourage participants to discuss ideas with each other, but the process is shorter and the analysis is not as extensive as in traditional focus groups. Their reports include summaries of the surveys and index card and roundtable exercises, as well as major findings from the discussion. They usually conduct the focus groups in capstone courses, and, depending on the size of the class, they run several simultaneous groups. This allows them to avoid many of the scheduling and recruitment problems that often plague focus group projects. Noel and his colleagues train student assistants to facilitate the groups and work with them to develop and pilot test the focus group questions. This system provides a win-win situation for students and for the campus. Students receive valuable training and experience in qualitative research, and the campus receives a useful assessment service.

Although group interviews can be conducted with groups of any size, traditional focus groups usually involve from six to ten participants. Having fewer participants can limit the variety of expressed viewpoints, but having more than ten decreases the opportunity for everyone to participate. Groups can be larger if less interaction is required, as in structured group interviews, but traditional focus groups rely heavily on group

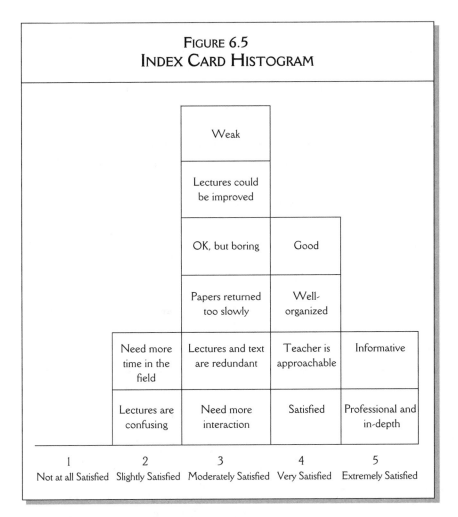

FIGURE 6.5
INDEX CARD HISTOGRAM

	Weak		
	Lectures could be improved		
	OK, but boring	Good	
	Papers returned too slowly	Well-organized	
Need more time in the field	Lectures and text are redundant	Teacher is approachable	Informative
Lectures are confusing	Need more interaction	Satisfied	Professional and in-depth

1	2	3	4	5
Not at all Satisfied	Slightly Satisfied	Moderately Satisfied	Very Satisfied	Extremely Satisfied

interaction. Group members should have a common level of experience that allows them to discuss the issues. For example, freshmen and seniors would not be a good mix because they would have very different perspectives, and the seniors would likely dominate the discussion. If the opinions of both freshmen and seniors are of interest, they should be interviewed in separate focus groups. It is important to select participants who have something to say about the relevant issues and who will be able to speak freely without being intimidated by others.

Facilitators often conduct more than one focus group to develop a thorough understanding of the issues being explored. A good rule of thumb is to continue collecting information until the groups become repetitive, giving facilitators confidence in their conclusions (Morgan & Krueger, 1998). Personal experience using focus groups for program assessment suggests that two to four focus groups usually are sufficient.

Focus group reports vary considerably in the amount of presented information. The person who prepares the report must be able to work with extensive amounts of qualitative information and must be perceived as someone who is professional and fair in dealing with the collected information. Some provide only a summary of findings, while others provide a summary of findings, transcripts on which the findings are based, and suggestions for how the findings can be used to improve the program. In all cases, researchers must maintain the confidentiality of the participants, and this requires a careful editing of transcripts and quotations included in the report. How the report will be written, who will receive the report, and when it will be completed should be clarified in advance to avoid misunderstandings.

Although their implementation may be time-consuming and skilled facilitators are needed, focus groups can provide important insights about programs. They have the potential to uncover unanticipated information that would not be captured by other assessment techniques.

REFLECTIVE ESSAYS

Reflective essay assignments invite students to reflect on some aspect of their university experience. Reflective essays can be administered in a number of ways and can collect feedback about programs or about the entire campus. Open-ended survey questions and course journals often call for brief reflective essays, and longer essays could be collected as in-class or homework writing assignments. Some campuses have required examinations to certify general education writing requirements, and reflective essays could be used to assess writing competence as well as to collect student feedback on selected issues. Students often are asked to include reflective essays in portfolios to discuss their strengths and weaknesses, their development as students, and their preparation for their anticipated career.

Reflective essays should be based on carefully crafted, open-ended questions. Here are some examples of reflective essay questions that could be used for program assessment:

- Describe the most valuable thing you learned in our program, and explain how this will be useful to you in your future.

- Which of the program's learning objectives are the most and least important to you? Why?

- Explain how you have grown as a person and as a nurse during your experience in the program. To what do you attribute your growth?

- Thinking about your experience in our program, describe how the program could be improved to increase your learning.

- Many students are understandably interested in preparing for a career. How might our program be changed to better prepare you for your anticipated career?

- Faculty vary in their teaching styles. What types of teaching have been particularly effective in helping you learn?

- Faculty have asked you to complete a number of group projects and activities. What did you learn about effective teamwork and how did you learn these lessons?

- Faculty are concerned that too many students do not complete reading assignments before coming to class. If you were an instructor at this university, how would you motivate your students to complete reading assignments?

- Reflect upon your experiences with diversity on our campus. What have your experiences taught you about diversity?

- How might the psychology club be improved to better serve your personal interests and goals?

- Explain why you selected the items for inclusion in your portfolio and what they reveal about your growth.

- Reflect upon the process of preparing your portfolio. Did it help you better understand yourself or your education at our campus? Explain.

When students are asked to reflect on their learning (e.g., to "Discuss how well the program helped you develop critical thinking skills"), reflective essays indirectly assess program learning objectives. Sometimes faculty can use reflective essays to directly assess student learning. For example, students could be asked to reflect on their service learning and to describe what they learned about themselves. Faculty could directly assess program learning objectives associated with the development of self-understanding by analyzing the depth of insight revealed in these essays.

Classroom assessment (Angelo & Cross, 1993) could be used to obtain student reflections about their programs. As mentioned in Chapter 5, classroom assessment techniques were designed to help faculty improve the instruction of specific courses, but they can be adapted for use in program assessment by aggregating results across the curriculum. For example, students could be asked to write an "exam or assignment evaluation" or to complete an "assignment reaction exercise" to help faculty improve the effectiveness of these activities, or students could participate in a "class opinion poll" to help faculty understand the impact of the curriculum on attitudes or values. Short email surveys with reflective essay questions might be valuable tools to collect quick feedback from students, and these might be particularly useful when class time cannot be devoted to assessment or when students are participating in distant learning courses. Responses could be sent to course instructors or to a neutral party if confidentiality is a concern.

Reflective essays provide students opportunities to make qualitative statements about their learning and to share ideas for program improvement, and they have the potential to help students clarify their opinions or develop personal insights. Because the assignments are open-ended, this technique allows faculty to discover new ideas that might otherwise have been overlooked.

SUMMARY OF INDIRECT ASSESSMENT TECHNIQUES

Each of the indirect assessment techniques described in this chapter has potential strengths and limitations, as summarized in Figure 6.6. This summary, combined with the one at the end of Chapter 5, might be useful to faculty as they select and implement assessment techniques.

	FIGURE 6.6 STRENTHS AND LIMITATIONS OF INDIRECT ASSESSMENT TECHNIQUES	
Technique	Potential Strengths	Potential Limitations
Surveys	• Are flexible in format and can include questions about many issues. • Can be administered to large groups of respondents. • Can easily assess the views of various stakeholders. • Usually have face validity–the questions generally have a clear relationship to the objectives being assessed. • Tend to be inexpensive to administer. • Can be conducted relatively quickly. • Responses to closed-ended questions are easy to tabulate and to report in tables or graphs. • Open-ended questions allow faculty to uncover unanticipated results. • Can be used to track opinions across time to explore trends. • Are amenable to different formats, such as paper-and-pencil or online formats. • Can be used to collect opinions from respondents at distant sites.	• Provide indirect evidence about student learning. • Their validity depends on the quality of the questions and response options. • Conclusions can be inaccurate if biased samples are obtained. • Results might not include the full array of opinions if the sample is small. • What people say they do or know may be inconsistent with what they actually do or know. • Open-ended responses can be difficult and time-consuming to analyze.
Interviews	• Are flexible in format and can include questions about many issues.	• Generally provide indirect evidence about student learning. *(continued on page 128)*

127

Technique	Potential Strengths	Potential Limitations
	• Can assess the views of various stakeholders. • Usually have face validity–the questions generally have a clear relationship to the objectives being assessed. • Can provide insights into the reasons for participants' beliefs, attitudes, and experiences. • Interviewers can prompt respondents to provide more detailed responses. • Interviewers can respond to questions and clarify misunderstandings. • Telephone interviews can be used to reach distant respondents. • Can provide a sense of immediacy and personal attention for respondents. • Open-ended questions allow faculty to uncover unanticipated results.	• Their validity depends on the quality of the questions. • Poor interviewer skills can generate limited or useless information. • Can be difficult to obtain a representative sample of respondents. • What people say they do or know may be inconsistent with what they actually do or know. • Can be relatively time-consuming and expensive to conduct, especially if interviewers and interviewees are paid or if the no-show rate for scheduled interviews is high. • The process can intimidate some respondents, especially if asked about sensitive information and their identity is known to the interviewer. • Results can be difficult and time-consuming to analyze. • Transcriptions of interviews can be time-consuming and costly.
Focus groups	• Are flexible in format and can include questions about many issues. • Can provide in-depth exploration of issues. • Usually have face validity–the questions generally have a clear relationship to the objectives being assessed.	• Generally provide indirect evidence about student learning. • Require a skilled, unbiased facilitator. • Their validity depends on the quality of the questions. • Results might not include the full array of opinions if only one focus group is conducted.

Technique	Potential Strengths	Potential Limitations
	• Can be combined with other techniques, such as surveys. • The process allows faculty to uncover unanticipated results. • Can provide insights into the reasons for participants' beliefs, attitudes, and experiences. • Can be conducted within courses. • Participants have the opportunity to react to each other's ideas, providing an opportunity to uncover the degree of consensus on ideas that emerge during the discussion.	• What people say they do or know may be inconsistent with what they actually do or know. • Recruiting and scheduling the groups can be difficult. • Time-consuming to collect and analyze data.
Reflective essays	• Are flexible in format and can collect information about many issues. • Can be administered to large groups of respondents. • Usually have face validity–the writing assignment generally has a clear relationship to the objectives being assessed. • Can be conducted relatively quickly. • Allow faculty to uncover unanticipated results. • Can provide in-depth information about participants' experiences, attitudes, and perspectives. • Can provide insights into the reasons for participants' beliefs, attitudes, and experiences. • Can provide direct assessment of some learning objectives.	• Generally provide indirect evidence about student learning. • Their validity depends on the quality of the questions. • Conclusions can be inaccurate if biased samples are obtained. • Results might not include the full array of opinions if the sample is small. • What people say they do or know may be inconsistent with what they actually do or know. • Responses can be difficult and time-consuming to analyze.

7

MAKING SENSE OF ASSESSMENT DATA

Imagine that faculty in your department collected assessment data using reflective essays, open-ended survey questions, embedded essay questions, or portfolios. You are sitting in your office, and in front of you is a set of these materials. Your task is to make sense of them. You want to summarize what has been learned, and you want to do this efficiently. Perhaps you are working alone, or maybe you are leading this effort and some faculty volunteers are waiting for your advice on how to proceed.

Collecting data is one thing, but making sense of them is something else. We want to use analytic techniques that are simple, direct, and effective. Faculty should focus on the task at hand. They are accustomed to pulling out red pens and covering student documents with wise advice. Analyzing data for program assessment is a much different task. The goals are to make sense of the information and to summarize it in a way that provides feedback on student mastery of learning objectives or that responds to questions that faculty want answered. In addition, the analysis should provide information that informs faculty as they decide how to respond to results. Focusing on these goals allows faculty to set down their red pens, tune out irrelevant information, and find efficient ways to complete the task—turning raw data into useful information.

Making sense of data takes time. Hastily thrown together data collection procedures may result in data that are not worth examining because results are ambiguous or unresponsive to the issues being addressed. Making sense of data is only part of a well-conceived assessment process. Data collection procedures should be pilot tested to ensure that they result in data that are worth analyzing.

This chapter describes two common ways to approach assessment data: content analysis and the use of rubrics. Content analysis allows us to summarize a communication. For example, we use content analysis to make sense of responses to open-ended survey questions. Rubrics allow us to categorize the quality of products, such as the quality of critical thinking in student essays. This chapter emphasizes basic approaches that faculty from any discipline can apply. While specialists may employ more sophisticated techniques, these simple strategies can yield information that contributes to meaningful, manageable, and sustainable assessment programs.

CONTENT ANALYSIS

Content analysis involves making sense of the material being reviewed. Most often this material will be verbal, such as interview or survey responses, but we might also want to describe themes that occur in products, such as works of art or political cartoons. Although one person can conduct a content analysis, results might have more credibility if multiple reviewers are involved. Idiosyncratic interpretations and preconceptions are less likely to influence results, and inter-rater agreement can be examined.

Content analysis should be approached with an open mind and a willingness to "hear" what respondents are saying. While everyone enjoys hearing praise, most faculty don't celebrate when they receive criticism. Reviewers should be aware that common responses to criticism are to defend or counterattack. They should avoid "spinning" results to support their personal opinions or denigrating those whose opinions differ from their own.

When approaching this task, faculty should begin with a clear understanding of the goals associated with the review. If they are examining responses to a survey question on the quality of advising, their content analysis should focus on what students report about advising. If they are reviewing student reflections on the impact of campus experiences on their ability to interact within a multicultural environment, the focus should be on identifying the types of experiences that students mention and the consequences of those experiences. Faculty should ask, "Why am I reviewing these materials? What do we want to learn?" The answers will direct the focus of the content analysis.

When conducting the content analysis, reviewers want to summarize common themes and the extent of consensus concerning those themes. Generally, they develop a written coding scheme that describes how individual responses will be categorized. Then they code data by recording instances of each category so they can develop accurate summaries in the reports. Coding results for small studies can be easily accomplished by hand, and a statistical program (e.g., SPSS) or spreadsheet (e.g., Excel) is often used to help organize results for larger studies.

Sometimes coding categories are predetermined. At other times categories emerge as materials are reviewed. For example, if students are asked about the quality of advising, three categories might be predetermined: negative, neutral, and positive. Readers could review each response and categorize it appropriately, and this probably could be done fairly rapidly.

If the content analysis stops at this point, however, readers have thrown away much potentially useful information. In fact, if faculty only wanted to learn how often students categorize advising experiences as negative, neutral, or positive, it would have been easier to use a simple item requesting this rating. Students were asked to write essays because more information was desired, and content analysis involves objectively summarizing this information. As reviewers analyze the content, themes emerge, and these are integrated into the coding scheme. For example, readers might notice that students who report negative experiences often complain about the lack of advisor availability in the evenings, or they may notice that students who report positive experiences often praise the peer advising center. This is information worth including in the summary because it adds to the formative validity of the assessment process.

Once the coding scheme is finalized, it can be applied to the documents. If multiple readers are involved, it is typical to ask them to independently review a few products so checks for inter-rater reliability can be conducted. If disagreements are rare, the process can continue, but if disagreements are common, readers should identify the reasons for the discrepancies and agree on how they should be resolved. In this way, they clarify ambiguities in the coding scheme.

Usually basic student information, such as gender and class level, is coded, too. This allows the reviewer to describe characteristics of the sample in the report, and the reviewer might decide to examine sub-group differences. For example, some themes might occur more often among women or among international students, and this added information may be important for using the results effectively. Try your hand at coding student responses in Figure 7.1.

Once data are coded, the summary should be written with the audience in mind. Program faculty want concise reports that address the questions they want answered. Exemplars should be provided for all themes that are discussed, so their meanings are clear; and sometimes reports provide complete lists of all comments related to each theme so readers can independently judge their meaning. If only exemplars are provided, conclusions should be quantified. For example, "Fifty percent of the students who report negative experiences requested evening advising hours." This quantification (50%) provides a summary that is much less ambiguous than using terms like "many" and "most." When faculty read that "Many students requested evening advising hours," it is not clear if "many" means three, 15, or 50 out of the 100 students who responded. Opinions that are expressed more frequently are more likely to be given serious attention.

Reports should include sufficient detail so that readers can interpret numerical results accurately. For example, if you report student suggestions for improving program advising, you might state that 80% of the students suggest one solution and 40% suggest an alternative solution. The alert reader will notice that these percentages sum to over 100%, and this might be confusing unless you have noted that students were allowed to offer multiple suggestions. In addition, the report should clarify how many responses were considered. For example, if only a fraction of the students offered suggestions, the report might say, "Forty percent of students offered suggestions for improving advising. Among these, 50% recommended that advisors be available in the evening." This is less ambiguous than simply reporting that 20% of students recommended evening advising. If counts are given, rather than percentages, they

FIGURE 7.1
CONTENT ANALYSIS CODING PRACTICE

Here is a coding scheme for student responses to this question: "Faculty want students in our program to develop search skills to identify and secure print and non-print materials relevant to topics in political science. Describe one assignment or activity that you experienced in a political science course that helped you strengthen these search skills."

Faculty asked this question because they wanted to hear students' perspective on which types of assignments and activities most effectively help them develop search skills. Based on reviewing a sample of student responses, faculty developed the following coding scheme:

1) Identification number (assign each student a number, beginning with "1")

2) Student class level (1 = Freshman, 2 = Sophomore, 3 = Junior, 4 = Senior, 5 = Grad)

3) Overall response (0 = no response/question was unanswered, 1 = provided a usable response, 2 = stated/implied that search skills were not strengthened in a P.S. course, 3 = response was not relevant to the question/could not be coded)

4) Positive mention of a structured assignment that leads students step-by-step through the search process (0 = No, 1 = Yes)

5) Positive mention of an assignment that required students to use or develop search skills, but no mention of step-by-step guidance (category 4) or group activity (category 6) (0 = No, 1 = Yes)

6) Positive mention of an assignment or activity that required working collaboratively with peers (0 = No, 1 = Yes)

7) Positive mention of a how-to-search lecture in a course (0 = No, 1 = Yes)

8) Positive mention of an in-class activity related to search skills (0 = No, 1 = Yes)

9) Positive mention of the use of online learning materials (0 = No, 1 = Yes)

10) Positive mention of personal assistance by a faculty member (0 = No, 1 = Yes)

11) Positive mention of personal assistance by a TA (0 = No, 1 = Yes)

12) Positive mention of personal assistance by a librarian (0 = No, 1 = Yes)

Use this scheme to code the responses below. Create a coding sheet with 12 columns (one column for each coding category) and five rows (one row for each student), and enter the appropriate code in each column.

(continued on page 136)

1) (a senior) "I think I learned the most when Professor Ruiz required team projects. We had to do a thorough literature review, and most of us didn't know how to start, but my team had a couple of students who were really good at computers, and we all learned a lot. We also really appreciated the help of Cindy, one of the reference librarians. She was always able to answer our questions when we got confused."

2) (a graduate student) "I thought I was pretty good at finding materials until I took Dr. Web's class. She made us break the search into steps: Clarify the research question, identify key terms, etc. This really helped me learn how to structure searches, and now I use these skills every time I need to find some information."

3) (a junior) "I had to do lit reviews for papers in several PS courses and learned how to do searches then. Sometimes I got help from the TA."

4) (a senior) "The first time I had to do a major lit review, I was totally lost. I went to Dr. Meese's office, and he showed me how to use the campus search system. Thanks, Dr. M.!"

5) (a sophomore) "I'm not very good at this. I kinda wander around the library looking at journals and books in the PS section until I find something I can use."

Here is the coding:
1 4 1 0 0 1 0 0 0 0 0 1
2 5 1 1 0 0 0 0 0 0 0 0
3 3 1 0 1 0 0 0 0 0 1 0
4 4 1 0 1 0 0 0 0 1 0 0
5 2 2 0 0 0 0 0 0 0 0 0

should be presented in a context that clarifies how many products were reviewed. For example, the fact that 20 students praised the peer advising center has different meaning if they were in a sample of 30 students or in a sample of 500 students.

Sprinkling reports with direct quotes from students—using the student's voice—makes the reports more powerful because the results clearly represent what students are telling us. Instead of wondering if the person doing the summary misrepresented student opinions, faculty are able to assess this themselves. If this is overdone, busy faculty will ignore quotations, but well-chosen quotations can have high impact. Although the following story is not from higher education, it illustrates this point in a memorable way. A friend worked under contract to examine the experiences of spouses of enlisted military personnel as part of a larger effort to examine operations at a military base. He delivered a long written report sparkling with tables of numbers, and he was invited to address high-ranking officers to summarize his findings. He used PowerPoint slides of his tables to support his main conclusions, then he reported on some focus groups and included a story shared by a young military wife whose baby almost died because ambulance drivers could not find a place to park near their on-base housing. The commanding officer immediately ordered his staff to find a solution, and it was quickly implemented. According to my friend, that one story had more impact on base functioning than all the rest of the report. People like to hear stories, and they often respond to them in different ways than they respond to the same types of information presented in neatly tabulated columns. This experience also points out the need for reviewers to attend to individual responses.

Sometimes an individual's response is unique and does not fit the coding scheme, but it is so important that it deserves recognition in the report. For example, if a disabled student in a focus group expresses concern about the safety of a campus bus ramp, this information should be provided to relevant campus personnel. Reports sometimes include lists of all comments because readers may decide that some of the points are of sufficient importance that they should be addressed, regardless of how often they occur.

The report also should provide other information that affects interpretation. For example, it should summarize characteristics of the sample. Readers will want to know if results are *generalizable*, that is, if they are likely to accurately represent all student opinions. Were the products from a representative sample of students or were they from a special sample, such as honors students or new transfer students? Findings from special samples may not accurately describe the opinions or experiences of other groups. Readers should have information on how the data were collected and how student privacy and confidentiality were addressed. Students might respond differently if they are interviewed by faculty who determine their grades, and they may withhold personal information if they believe responses can be tied to them. Content analysis allows you to summarize what was found, but the entire process should be designed to provide valid information.

SCORING RUBRICS

Assessment workshop participants often report that the segment on rubrics had the greatest impact on their assessment activities, as well as their teaching. Scoring rubrics make the impossible manageable.

Scoring rubrics are explicit schemes for classifying products or behaviors into categories that are steps along a continuum. These steps generally range from "unacceptable" to "exemplary," and the number of intermediate categories varies with the need to discriminate among other performance levels. Rubrics can be used to classify virtually any product or behavior, such as essays, research reports, portfolios, works of art, recitals, oral presentations, performances, and group activities. Judgments can include self-assessments by students or judgments can be made by others, such as faculty, other students, fieldwork supervisors, and external reviewers. Rubrics are versatile tools. They can be used to provide formative feedback to students, to grade students, and to assess programs. A well-designed rubric should allow evaluators to efficiently focus on specific learning objectives while reviewing complex student products, such as theses, without getting bogged down in irrelevant details.

There are two major types of scoring rubrics: *holistic* and *analytic*. Holistic rubrics describe how one global, holistic judgment is made. Analytic rubrics involve making a series of judgments, each assessing a characteristic of the product being evaluated. Figure 7.2 is a holistic rubric, and Figure 7.3 is an analytic rubric. As you read these rubrics, think about how you might adapt them for your own use.

Notice that the descriptions in the holistic rubric combine various dimensions, such as focus, development, and the use of language. Holistic judgments are made based on reviewing the entire product in sufficient detail so that the classification can be made with confidence. This allows readers to scan complicated products, such as portfolios, paying careful attention only to segments directly related to making this discrimination. Professional readers, such as readers who review essays for test publishers, can make holistic judgments concerning student writing quickly and with substantial reliability and validity. Faculty, with some practice, can develop similar skills.

The rubric in Figure 7.3 engages students in the assessment by asking them to rate peers who developed team projects together. Sharing

FIGURE 7.2
HOLISTIC RUBRIC FOR ASSESSING STUDENT ESSAYS

Inadequate	The essay has at least one serious weakness. It may be unfocused, underdeveloped, or rambling. Problems with the use of language seriously interfere with the reader's ability to understand what is being communicated.
Developing competence	The essay may be somewhat unfocused, underdeveloped, or rambling, but it does have some coherence. Problems with the use of language occasionally interfere with the reader's ability to understand what is being communicated.
Acceptable	The essay is generally focused and contains some development of ideas, but the discussion may be simplistic or repetitive. The language lacks syntactic complexity and may contain occasional grammatical errors, but the reader is able to understand what is being communicated.
Sophisticated	The essay is focused and clearly organized, and it shows depth of development. The language is precise and shows syntactic variety, and ideas are clearly communicated to the reader.

FIGURE 7.3
ANALYTIC RUBRIC FOR PEER ASSESSMENT OF TEAM PROJECT MEMBERS

	Below Expectation	Good	Exceptional
Project contributions	Made few substantive contributions to the team's final product	Contributed a "fair share" of substance to the team's final product	Contributed considerable substance to the team's final product
Leadership	Rarely or never exercised leadership	Accepted a "fair share" of leadership responsibilities	Routinely provided excellent leadership
Collaboration	Undermined group discussions or often failed to participate	Respected others' opinions and contributed to the group's discussion	Respected others' opinions and made major contributions to the group's discussion

this rubric with students early in the term gives them guidance on faculty expectations, and sometimes such rubrics are developed in consultation with the students themselves. Programs often have interpersonal skills among their learning objectives, but many faculty are not comfortable trying to teach these skills because they have no special training in this area. A rubric such as this could help faculty structure expectations and provide students with appropriate feedback, and it could help faculty align the curriculum with this objective and collect data for program assessment. Rubrics have many uses.

Analytic rubrics can be thought of as collections of holistic rubrics that assess different aspects of the product being assessed. These aspects should be linked to learning objectives, and they may be developed through primary trait analysis (Walvoord & Anderson, 1998). Primary trait analysis is the process of determining the primary traits (criteria) that faculty use to evaluate products. The rubric in Figure 7.3 assesses three primary traits: project contributions, leadership, and collaboration.

The previous examples describe categories, but rubrics also can be used to generate scores. Figure 7.4 is a rubric that could be used for grading oral presentations. The rubric includes possible score ranges for each cell, and total scores can range from 0 to 30. If a rubric like this is embedded in lower-division and upper-division courses, faculty could track student growth in these skills. Using rubrics as embedded assessment tools should not interfere with faculty control of their classes or grading practices. As was mentioned in Chapter 1, grading requires more precise measurement than assessment. Although faculty may agree to share a common rubric, each might add additional course-specific traits and each might assign points to the categories in different ways. The scores on this rubric could be used for grading, but the categories that were used might provide sufficient detail for program assessment.

Rubrics can be created for examining almost any product, including portfolios. Figure 7.5 is a generic rubric for assessing learning objectives using portfolios. Notice the emphasis on evidence, rather than conjecture. This rubric might provide sufficient guidance for faculty reviewers, or they may need more detailed criteria for some learning objectives. Perhaps a generic rubric would be useful as a starting point, when faculty first review portfolios, and discussion will lead to the development of a

FIGURE 7.4
ANALYTIC RUBRIC FOR GRADING
ORAL PRESENTATIONS

	Below Expectation	Satisfactory	Exemplary	Score
Organization	No apparent organization. Evidence is not used to support assertions. (0-2)	The presentation has a focus and provides some evidence that supports conclusions. (3-5)	The presentation is carefully organized and provides convincing evidence to support conclusions. (6-8)	
Content	The content is inaccurate or overly general. Listeners are unlikely to learn anything or may be misled. (0-2)	The content is generally accurate, but incomplete. Listeners may learn some isolated facts, but they are unlikely to gain new insights about the topic. (5-7)	The content is accurate and complete. Listeners are likely to gain new insights about the topic. (10-13)	
Style	The speaker appears anxious and uncomfortable, and reads notes, rather than speaks. Listeners are largely ignored. (0-2)	The speaker is generally relaxed and comfortable, but too often relies on notes. Listeners are sometimes ignored or misunderstood. (3-6)	The speaker is relaxed and comfortable, speaks without undue reliance on notes, and interacts effectively with listeners. (7-9)	
Total Score				

more detailed rubric. If faculty always wait until they perfect procedures, little assessment would occur!

Program assessment using rubrics can be conducted in a number of ways. Faculty can use rubrics in classes and aggregate the data across sections, faculty can independently assess student products and then aggregate results, or faculty can participate in group readings in which they

FIGURE 7.5
GENERIC RUBRIC FOR ASSESSING PORTFOLIOS

	Unacceptable: Evidence that the student has mastered this objective is not provided, unconvincing, or very incomplete.	Marginal: Evidence that the student has mastered this objective is provided, but it is weak or incomplete.	Acceptable: Evidence shows that the student has generally attained this objective.	Exceptional: Evidence demonstrates that the student has mastered this objective at a high level.
Learning Objective 1				
Learning Objective 2				
Learning Objective 3				

review student products together and discuss what they found. Group readings can be very effective. Faculty often develop deeper understanding of the learning objectives and refine the rubric as they work, and they can immediately discuss the implications of results with the evidence fresh in their minds. Field work supervisors or community professionals also may be invited to assess student work using rubrics, and sometimes students are invited to do self or peer assessments.

Rubrics should be pilot tested, and evaluators should be "*normed*" or "*calibrated*" before they apply them. This is often accomplished through training using sample products that are established exemplars of different levels of performance. If group readings are conducted, they generally begin with everyone independently reviewing a few products so that differences can be discussed and resolved. If two evaluators apply the rubric to each product, inter-rater reliability can be examined. Once the data are collected, faculty discuss results to identify program strengths and areas of concern, then they close the loop by identifying and making changes to improve student learning.

Sometimes faculty readers require special training to overcome old habits. Faculty who are accustomed to grading on a curve might have difficulty making judgments based on the criteria stated in a rubric. They need to know that it is not essential to use all rubric levels and that they should not be concerned about how often each category is used. Some learning objectives are easier to achieve than others or are better aligned with the curriculum, so it is possible to find extensive use of higher categories for some objectives and lower categories for other objectives. The assessment should uncover student strengths, as well as limitations, and conclusions should be based on an objective application of the criteria stated in the rubric. Readers also should be told to be careful to rate each category in analytic rubrics separately, avoiding a *halo effect*. A halo effect occurs when judgments are influenced by each other. For example, if students are asked to use the peer assessment rubric in Figure 7.3, they might be tempted to classify an uncooperative student into the lowest category on all three dimensions, even if only one is appropriate.

Although this book does not focus on grading, rubrics often are embedded in courses because they are so useful for this purpose. As was mentioned in Chapter 1, learner-centered teaching often uses collaborative and cooperative learning models to help students develop, and these models work best when students are not penalized for working together. Rubrics allow faculty to assign grades based on the achievement of objectives rather than on how well students perform compared to each other, so their use encourages students to help each other learn. Figure 7.6 offers some suggestions for using rubrics in courses. Faculty can get double duty out of rubrics by using one rubric for grading *and* program assessment.

Holistic rubrics can be created using seven steps:

1) Identify what you are assessing (e.g., critical thinking).

2) Identify the characteristics of what you are assessing (e.g., appropriate use of evidence, recognition of logical fallacies).

3) Describe the best work you could expect using these characteristics. This describes the top category.

4) Describe the worst acceptable product using these characteristics. This describes the lowest acceptable category.

5) Describe an unacceptable product. This describes the lowest category.

6) Develop descriptions of intermediate-level products and assign them to intermediate categories. You might decide to develop a

---

FIGURE 7.6
SUGGESTIONS FOR USING RUBRICS IN COURSES

- Hand out the grading rubric with the assignment so students will know your expectations and how they'll be graded. This should help students master your learning objectives by guiding their work in appropriate directions.

- Use a rubric for grading student work and return the rubric with the grading on it. Faculty save time writing extensive comments; they just circle or highlight relevant segments of the rubric. Some faculty include room for additional comments on the rubric page, either within each section or at the end.

- Develop a rubric with your students for an assignment or group project. Students can then monitor themselves and their peers using agreed-upon criteria that they helped develop. Many faculty find that students create higher standards for themselves than faculty would impose on them.

- Have students apply your rubric to some sample products before they create their own. Faculty report that students are quite accurate when doing this, and this process should help them evaluate their own products as they are being developed. The ability to evaluate, edit, and improve draft documents is an important skill.

- Have students exchange paper drafts and give peer feedback using the rubric; then give students a few days before the final drafts are turned in to you. You might also require that they turn in the draft and scored rubric with their final paper.

- Have students self-assess their products using the grading rubric and hand in the self-assessment with the product; then faculty and students can compare self- and faculty-generated evaluations.

---

scale with five levels (e.g., unacceptable, marginal, acceptable, competent, outstanding), three levels (e.g., novice, competent, exemplary), or any other set that is meaningful.

7) Ask colleagues who were not involved in the rubric's development to apply it to some products or behaviors and revise as needed to eliminate ambiguities.

These steps can be repeated to generate an analytic rubric. The first time you try to create a rubric is the hardest, but, like any skill, it becomes easier with practice.

Developing a rubric takes time, and sometimes it is easier to adapt one that already exists. Fortunately, many examples are available. Walvoord and Anderson's (1998) book, *Effective Grading*, and Wiggins's (1998) book, *Educative Assessment*, include many rubrics, and the information literacy rubrics developed by the Colorado Department of Education (http://www.cde.state.co.us/cdelib/download/pdf/inforubr.pdf) cover a wide range of important learning objectives. Many others are available on the web, and links to them are available on the California State University Student Learning Outcomes site (http://www.calstate. edu/acadaff/sloa/links/rubrics.shtml).

As you look for rubrics to adapt, keep an open mind. Look for general formats, relevant concepts, and key words that you can incorporate into your work. Don't restrict yourself to rubrics created for your discipline. Faculty in an economics program might find that a rubric designed for assessing students' mastery of basketball dribbling is almost perfect. They just have to replace "dribble the ball" with "apply Keynesian economics." In addition, don't ignore the potential of rubrics developed for primary and secondary schools. Many can be easily adapted to higher education by strengthening requirements. Your goal when examining others' rubrics is not to find one that you can apply directly to your work; look for ideas that help you customize a rubric to match your needs.

INTER-RATER RELIABILITY

We generally want to verify that scores based on subjective judgments have inter-rater reliability. Inter-rater reliability indicates the extent of agreement among different reviewers. Without this information, we might wonder if summaries are accurate depictions of what was examined. For example, if we knew that a content analysis was done by a faculty member who is skeptical about the value of virtual courses, we might be suspicious of this person's summary of student opinions on this topic. If other raters agree, though, we have more confidence in the conclusions. This section describes some simple ways to examine inter-rater reliability. As with content analysis and rubrics, basic strategies that could be applied by anyone are described. Experts may conduct more sophisticated analyses, but usually these are not necessary if the only purpose is to verify that results are reasonably reliable.

When we do content analyses, subjective judgments are involved in two steps: establishing the themes to be coded and doing the coding. Probably the best way to have confidence in the selected themes is to have at least two people independently develop them, compare notes, and come to agreement. This process can be summarized in the report, and readers could be told how difficult it was to determine the final categories. To examine inter-rater reliability of coding judgments, we need to have at least two readers independently apply the coding scheme to a set of documents so we can compare their judgments. Content analyses frequently involve dichotomous decisions: Is the variable being coded present or not? In this case, the percentage of agreements is a good indicator of inter-rater reliability. Do the raters agree 10% of the time or is this percentage closer to 90%? Ten percent is too low; most would agree that 90% is acceptable, although even higher would be better. Figure 7.7 demonstrates this calculation. The finding of 70% agreement in this example suggests that the criteria for identifying the presence of this theme are too loosely defined and further work is needed. Coding schemes should be pilot tested and checked for inter-rater reliability *before* faculty invest time in coding the entire data set.

An alternative approach is to have pairs of raters work together on all decisions, collaborating as they go to resolve discrepancies. Although judgments probably are made more slowly, raters generally are very confident about their accuracy. To examine this process, you might ask pairs of raters to keep track of how often they disagreed in their original judgments. If this percentage is low, you probably could reduce the workload by having only one rater analyze each product. You also, of course, could have two pairs of raters analyze the same set of documents and calculate the percentage of their agreements. In this way, you treat each pair of raters as if they were one person.

You may recognize that these calculations have a flaw. You could get perfect inter-rater agreement if both raters always use one rating category, that is, always code that the theme is absent or that the theme is present. This could happen when themes occur in almost no products or in almost every product. The purpose of the assessment is to uncover findings that will inform decision-making. It is important, of course, to report information that has considerable consensus, and sometimes it is useful to report a rare, but significant event (such as the story of the baby at the military base). The percentage-of-agreement summary statistic is most reasonable when many opportunities for disagreement occur, and this happens when we examine themes that are common but not universal.

Figure 7.7
Calculating the Percentage of Agreements

Here are coding results for two raters who made dichotomous decisions about the presence of a theme in ten products. A "0" indicates that the theme is absent; a "1" indicates that the theme is present.

0 0
0 0
0 1
0 1
1 0
1 1
1 1
1 1
1 1
1 1

Overall, the raters agreed seven times. They agreed two times that the theme was absent, and they agreed five times that the theme was present. They disagreed three times. They agreed on seven out of the ten judgments, so their percentage of agreement is 70%.

If judgments involve more than two categories, as is common in the use of scoring rubrics, the situation is a bit more complex. Two approaches are possible. First, one could assign scores to categories (e.g., "1" for the lowest of five categories and "5" for the highest), and then calculate the correlation between two raters who have reviewed a set of materials. This might work fine, but would fail if there is insufficient variability. Correlations summarize how much variability in one variable can be explained by the other. If most ratings use a single category, there may be insufficient variability to explain, and the correlation will be small–not because raters disagreed, but because the products being evaluated were too similar. An alternative is to ask how many of the ratings were identical, one point apart, two points apart, etc. For example, if a scoring rubric has five categories, judgments can be, at most, four points apart (one rater classifies the product in the lowest category and the other classifies it in the highest category). Say raters are identical on 80% of their ratings, within one point on 18% of their ratings, and within two points on the remaining 2% of the ratings. Most probably would find this acceptable. As with dichotomous judgments, raters could work in pairs, resolving discrepancies as they go, and you could examine the percentage of discrepancies requiring discussion or the degree of agreement between independent pairs of raters.

Figure 7.8 illustrates these calculations. In this example, raters gave identical ratings 75% of the time, differed by one point 20% of the time, and differed by two points 5% of the time, that is, ratings were within one point 95% of the time. Sometimes the distinction between selected categories is particularly important. For example, ratings of "1" and "2" might identify products that fall below minimum standards, and ratings of "3" and "4" might identify products that meet minimum standards. With only one exception (the product categorized as a "2" by one rater and as a "4" by the other rater), the raters agreed every time if a product met minimum expectations. Based on this analysis, the raters might agree to revisit this one product and come to consensus on it. The correlation for these data is .79. This summarizes the relationship in a different way, and the .79 is a moderately high correlation. Perfect agreement would generate a correlation of 1.0, and strong inter-rater reliability would be indicated by correlations in the .90s. These correlations must be interpreted loosely because they are affected by the amount of variability in scores. When using a 4-point rubric, variation might be low, which could reduce the size of the maximum possible correlation that could be observed.

MANAGING THE REVIEW

Sometimes one person does a content analysis or develops and applies a rubric, and other times these are team efforts. One of the most valuable aspects of program assessment is that it provides a forum for faculty discussion of student learning. At some point, all or most faculty in the program should find out what was learned and should discuss the implications for program functioning. It is not essential that everyone become involved in a content analysis or use a rubric, but the participation of more than one person can be useful. Their collective wisdom might make the process more reliable and valid, and each might learn from the experience.

Content analysis is often done by one person. Sometimes this person is a neutral outsider, such as an assessment consultant, but sometimes

---

FIGURE 7.8
SUMMARIZING THE DIFFERENCES BETWEEN RATINGS

Here are coding results for two raters who classify 20 products into four categories (labeled from "1" to "4").

```
1 1
1 1
1 2
2 1
2 2
2 2
2 2
2 4
3 3
3 3
3 3
3 3
3 3
3 3
3 3
4 3
4 3
4 4
4 4
4 4
```

In reviewing these 20 documents, the raters gave identical ratings 15 times (75%), disagreed by one point four times (20%), and disagreed by two points one time (5%). The correlation between the two sets of ratings is .79.

---

the task requires insider knowledge. In this case, a well-supervised undergraduate or graduate student may be able to do the job well. Having a large group create the coding scheme probably is a waste of time because most content analyses do not require this amount of collaboration, but inviting a second person to independently develop themes or pilot test the coding makes good sense. If coding criteria do not require high-level professional judgments, students may be able to do the coding with appropriate supervision. Whichever way it is done, it is important that the summary accurately reflects what was being analyzed and provides information with formative value. Faculty time is valuable, and their time may be best spent reflecting on a well-written summary and deciding what follow-up action is required.

Rubrics must be clearly written so they can provide reliable, valid information. If rubrics will be embedded within courses, involvement by faculty who offer these courses makes good sense, although most will serve on a consultative basis rather than as the rubrics' primary author. In addition, if the rubric is designed to assess a program learning objective, all program faculty have some interest in its development. This process should be inclusive, with open invitations for input by all relevant faculty.

Faculty have developed a number of strategies for applying rubrics to products. Sometimes faculty work alone. If assessments are embedded within courses, faculty may apply rubrics to student work within their own courses and send their results to someone who tabulates the data. Faculty also can independently apply rubrics to collected products. For example, program faculty may divide a collection of portfolios, with each faculty member assessing a portion of them. This can work well, but validity would be threatened if individuals apply standards differently. Training and norming generally are necessary to ensure the integrity of this process.

Rubrics often are applied by groups who come together for this purpose. For example, program faculty may agree to devote a half day to this task. Before the meeting, the rubric must be finalized, the products to be examined must be collected, and a data collection procedure must be developed. The reading should begin with an orientation to clarify the nature of the task and to norm the reviewers. Figure 7.9 offers some suggestions to the person who facilitates this orientation.

Group ratings can be collected in several ways. If the reliability of the rubric is known to be high, it may be reasonable to have only one reader analyze each document, but it generally is preferable to use two readers. Inter-rater reliability can be examined and errors can more easily be identified and corrected. When two readers work independently, the second reader may be allowed to peek at the first rater's judgments. Readers often are curious about other's opinions, and no harm is done if the first rater's scores are hidden until after the second opinions have been recorded. Sometimes results are monitored as they are turned in, and documents are given to a third reader when necessary to resolve discrepancies. For example, the facilitator may send any document that has a scorer difference of more than one point to a third reader who deter-

FIGURE 7.9
SCORING RUBRIC GROUP ORIENTATION

1) Invite readers who offer and control the curriculum and who have the capacity to make informed judgments about student learning.

2) Describe the purpose for the review, stressing how it fits into program assessment plans. Explain that the purpose is to assess the program, not individual students or faculty, and describe ethical guidelines, including respect for confidentiality and privacy.

3) Describe the nature of the products that will be reviewed, briefly summarizing how they were obtained.

4) Describe the scoring rubric and its categories. Explain how it was developed.

5) Explain that readers should rate each dimension of an analytic rubric separately, and they should apply the criteria without concern for how often each category is used.

6) Give each reviewer a copy of several student products that are exemplars of different levels of performance. Include, if possible, a weak product, an intermediate-level product, and a strong product, and you also might include a product that appears to be particularly difficult to judge. Ask each volunteer to independently apply the rubric to each of these products, and show them how to record their ratings.

7) Once everyone is done, collect everyone's ratings and display them so everyone can see the degree of agreement. This is often done on a blackboard, with each person in turn announcing his or her ratings as they are entered on the board. Alternatively, the facilitator could ask raters to raise their hands when their rating category is announced, making the extent of agreement very clear to everyone and making it very easy to identify raters who routinely give unusually high or low ratings.

8) Guide the group in a discussion of their ratings. There will be differences, and this discussion is important to establish standards. Attempt to reach consensus on the most appropriate rating for each of the products being examined by inviting people who gave different ratings to explain their judgments. Usually consensus is possible, but sometimes a split decision is developed. For example, the group may agree that a product is a "3-4" split because it has elements of both categories. Expect more discussion time if you include a hard-to-rate example, but its consideration might save time and prevent frustration during the subsequent review. You might allow the group to revise the rubric to clarify its use, but avoid allowing the group to drift away from the learning objective being assessed.

9) Once the group is comfortable with the recording form and the rubric, distribute the products and begin the data collection.

mines which rating is more accurate. Sometimes readers work in pairs, independently rating each document, then jointly resolving all disagreements. They may be asked to discuss only the ratings that differ by some amount, such as at least two units. When two raters disagree, faculty must decide which rating will be used in the analysis, or they may decide to use both (e.g., Allen, Moe, & Roberts, 2000; Noel, 2001a). Whatever the decision, the project report should document how data were generated.

Faculty often are in the best position to apply scoring rubrics, and they may be more likely to take results seriously if they conducted the analysis themselves. Others, however, may be invited to participate. Sometimes student self assessments have credibility, especially if based on objectively defined rubrics. Peers who have firsthand knowledge of relevant information also can apply rubrics, such as the peer rubric in Figure 7.3. Others may have expertise or firsthand knowledge, such as graduate students, fieldwork supervisors, alumni, or other professionals. Program faculty also might consider working with colleagues from institutions with similar missions. They could assess student work together, perhaps examining products from both campuses simultaneously, or they could review each other's student work. This might create opportunities to develop fresh ideas about curriculum and pedagogy, and it might lead to other collaborations, such as faculty exchanges, co-authored publications, or jointly sponsored theses. If they share rubrics, they also may be able to provide benchmark data that would be useful when interpreting findings. The need to provide training and to examine inter-rater agreement is important when people who did not participate in rubric development will assess student work. Rubrics are simple tools. They have many uses, and their value is limited only by the imaginations of those who use them.

8

PUTTING IT ALL TOGETHER

R emember the story of the boy at the beginning of Chapter 1–the boy who was proud that he was teaching his dog to talk, but who was unconcerned about whether his dog actually learned to speak? This is not how professional educators function. Program faculty identify what students should learn, align curricula and courses with those objectives, examine student learning, and make appropriate adjustments. A national study of department quality assurance practices, however, painted a distressing picture:

> Most departments and most faculty failed to see the relevance of program evaluation and assessment to the work they did. The dominant mood on the campuses we studied was that program review and other forms of departmental assessment are largely ritualistic and time-consuming affairs, mandated from above, having few real consequences for the lives of faculty. (Wergin, 1999, ¶ 5)

Fortunately, these findings were not universal. Researchers found that institutions with effective departmental reviews have a positive culture that supports meaningful assessment, policies that are viewed as credible and fair, and practices that pay careful attention to the quality of the evidence supporting decisions (Wergin, 1999). Institutions with effective programs have flexible, decentralized policies that empower faculty to define their missions, objectives, stakeholders, and assessment strategies. They recognize that program assessment should be faculty controlled.

LEARNER-CENTERED PROGRAMS

Assessment is an integral component of learner-centered education. Figure 8.1 contrasts teacher-centered and learner-centered models. Although these approaches are described as opposites, faculty are likely to include elements of both in their courses and curricula. As they become more learner-centered, instructors move from covering content to helping students master learning objectives. This transition can have profound impact on how faculty structure their courses and curricula, and generally leads to increased interest in depth of processing rather than breadth of coverage. Faculty design learning environments that engage students in their learning, and students construct deep understanding by reflecting on their learning and by discussing it with others. Students are encouraged to be intentional learners, and faculty routinely assess their impact on students, allowing them to improve courses and programs.

Learning objectives define how students demonstrate their mastery of what faculty want them to learn. Objectives are based on program mission and goals, and they clarify the desired depth of processing. Learner-centered faculty rely on course and program learning objectives to guide course and curriculum planning, grading, and assessment. Grading indicates how well course learning objectives have been mastered, and faculty use a variety of pedagogies to try to help all students meet these standards. Faculty abandon a gatekeeper role and the expectation that a normal distribution of test scores is desirable. Although they want all students to master the learning objectives, they recognize that they share responsibility for student development with fellow faculty, other campus professionals, and students themselves. Faculty accept responsibility for understanding how learning occurs and for creating effective learning environments, and they assess their impact on learners and seek ways to improve what they're doing.

Alignment is a key assessment concept. A cohesive curriculum is aligned with program learning objectives—it is designed to systematically introduce and develop student mastery of program objectives. Courses

154

FIGURE 8.1
TEACHING-CENTERED VERSUS
LEARNING-CENTERED INSTRUCTION

Concept	Teacher-Centered	Learner-Centered
Teaching goals	• Cover the discipline.	Students learn: • How to use the discipline. • How to integrate disciplines to solve complex problems. • An array of core learning objectives, such as communication and information literacy skills.
Organization of the curriculum	• Courses in catalog.	• Cohesive program with systematically created opportunities to synthesize, practice, and develop increasingly complex ideas, skills, and values.
Course structure	• Faculty cover topics.	• Students master learning objectives.
How students learn	• Listening. • Reading. • Independent learning, often in competition for grades.	• Students construct knowledge by integrating new learning into what they already know. • Learning is viewed as a cognitive and social act.
Pedagogy	• Based on delivery of information.	• Based on engagement of students.
Course delivery	• Lecture. • Assignments and exams for summative purposes.	• Active learning. • Assignments for formative purposes. • Collaborative learning. • Community service learning. • Cooperative learning. • Online, asynchronous, self-directed learning. • Problem-based learning.

(continued on page 156)

Concept	Teacher-Cenetered	Learner-Centered
Course grading	• Faculty as gatekeepers. • Normal distribution expected.	• Grades indicate mastery of learning objectives.
Faculty role	• Sage on the stage.	• Designer of learning environments.
Effective teaching	• Teach (present information) well and those who can will learn.	• Engage students in their learning. • Help all students master learning objectives. • Use classroom assessment to improve courses. • Use program assessment to improve programs.

are designed for this cohesive curriculum by aligning course objectives with program objectives. Course activities and grading are aligned with course objectives—to offer students feedback, motivation, and opportunities to learn. Student support staff and faculty align their efforts to support student development. Individual contributions are integrated into a complex, interdependent system that focuses on student development, and educational effectiveness is everyone's goal.

Learner-centered institutions are marked by ongoing communication, the use of evidence to guide decision-making, and a willingness to examine the impact of campus programs on students. This requires effective leadership, appropriate use of rewards and incentives, and ongoing support for faculty and staff development.

ASSESSMENT PLANNING

Assessment is not rocket science. Its major requirement is formative validity, and data need not be perfect to have heuristic value. Good assessment leads to faculty reflection and action to improve student learning. Faculty who treat potential data providers and each other with respect and who plan a series of simple, manageable studies are likely to find the experience intellectually engaging and productive.

Assessment programs are likely to fail if faculty and administrators forget the purpose of their efforts. Assessment studies examine student learning in the entire program; they should not focus on individual students or faculty. The purpose is not to assign blame, but rather to identify program strengths, areas of concern, and solutions that faculty are willing to implement.

Assessment involves collecting direct and indirect evidence concerning student development. Assessment studies might confirm that students meet all faculty expectations, and faculty can, based on these empirical findings, conclude that all is going well. More likely, faculty will find mixed results. Students will meet or exceed expectations for some objectives, but not others. Results can be surprising. According to *The Assessment Almanac 1997*, from Truman State University, "The key is whether the numbers shake you out of your complacency. We all thought we were good before, but the numbers convinced us that we needed to make changes in the curriculum and in the way we designed student questions and assignments" (p. III-6). Faculty should plan assessments in which they have confidence. Disappointing results should have sufficient credibility to "shake" faculty into action, and authentic assessments generally have high face and formative validity.

Three major criteria apply to assessment planning. Assessment should be meaningful, manageable, and sustainable. The focus should be on learning objectives that faculty value and that their curriculum supports. Faculty need not assess every learning objective in every student every year. Instead, they should develop a flexible, multiyear plan that results in incremental improvement. Assessment is an ongoing activity, and it is as much a part of the faculty role as mentoring students and teaching courses. Assessment is a "fundamental faculty responsibility" (Lopez, 1999, p. 14).

Embedding assessment in the curriculum has many advantages. Faculty examine learning where it occurs, students are motivated to demonstrate their learning, and assessment planning contributes to an aligned curriculum. Faculty can embed single exam questions, entire tests, in-class activities, fieldwork activities, and homework assignments that are designed to reflect how well students have mastered learning objectives. Faculty can collect this evidence to assess the program, and they can ask students to reflect on their learning, perhaps within reflective essays or portfolios which document their achievements.

A recurring theme in assessment is collaboration. Faculty work together to develop consensus on learning objectives, curriculum alignment, and assessment, and they collaborate to determine the implications of results. This requires collegiality, trust, and flexibility, and it requires program faculty to regularly discuss student learning. These conversations are an essential component of effective assessment. In addition, faculty collaborate with other campus professionals to develop a supportive learning environment. As national assessment leaders Catherine Palomba and Trudy Banta (1999) conclude, "Much of the value of assessment comes from the systematic way it makes educators question, discuss, share, and observe" (p. 328). Assessment is not a one-person enterprise.

It is likely that some program faculty will prefer not to participate in assessment activities, just as some faculty choose not to engage in research, community service, integrating the latest technology into their courses, or academic governance. Assessment is the responsibility of all program faculty, but the assessment workload can be distributed unevenly. Faculty have different strengths and interests, and programs require many types of professional service. Individuals or teams who accept major assessment responsibilities should be recognized for their contributions, and all faculty should cooperate when program-wide decisions are made. Faculty who sit on the sidelines may become more interested in assessment when they see that the process can be manageable and productive.

ESTABLISHING STANDARDS

Faculty generally set their own standards when they do program assessment. The standards allow them to decide if assessment results are satisfactory or if they suggest a problem that requires their attention.

Faculty should take the campus and program mission into account when they establish standards. Those who offer elite programs with a primary mission to prepare undergraduates for doctoral work probably have different expectations than faculty whose programs emphasize terminal undergraduate degrees. This argues against norm-referenced comparisons based on state or national standards. Such comparisons could lead to unfair conclusions about campuses which reach out to underprepared learners and which have missions that stress value-added objectives.

Rubrics are frequently used in assessment projects, and faculty must decide how to interpret their findings. They should not expect all students to be in the highest category of most rubrics. Students develop many competencies, and each student develops in unique ways. For example, some social work students will develop outstanding interpersonal skills and others will be stronger in interpreting the law. Faculty expect all students to develop learning objectives at some minimum level, but they should recognize that only rare students will excel in every way. The standards might indicate that basic requirements have been met if all students demonstrate minimum competence and if at least some fraction of them (e.g., 10%) demonstrate exceptional learning.

Sometimes faculty want to know how their students compare to students on other campuses, and they set expectations based on the relative performance of their students. For example, they may be disappointed if their average graduate scored below 500 on the relevant Major Field Test. Test publishers generally provide norms for different types of institutions, such as community colleges, liberal arts colleges, and comprehensive universities. If the test aligns with program learning objectives and curricula, comparisons with appropriate norm groups provide an external benchmark and opportunities for faculty to evaluate and confirm their overall standards. If the test does not align with the program, this approach would not be meaningful.

Faculty at campuses with similar missions could collaborate on the assessment of common learning objectives, giving them an opportunity to develop their own benchmarks. Creating and applying a rubric to student products might help faculty clarify their standards, and blind review of documents (e.g., reviewing collective portfolios without knowing the campus of origin) would allow faculty to confirm their standards and compare their students to others at similar institutions. This gives faculty the opportunity to verify that the students in their program will be competitive after graduation. Lopez (1999) highly recommends this procedure and concludes that these benchmarks might serve as external drivers for faculty on campuses with lower standards than their counterparts. Programs at the same institution with common learning objectives also could apply this strategy. For example, social science programs probably have a number of learning objectives that could be examined simultaneously, allowing faculty to develop shared internal benchmarks.

SUPPORT

Pressures to integrate new pedagogies into courses, continuing changes in technology, and an increasingly diverse student body demand faculty time. College and university faculty, always challenged to stay current in their disciplines, are now expected to contribute to learner-centered programs and to prepare students for a future that may make today's world look like the horse-and-buggy days of our predecessors. These are turbulent times in higher education.

Most faculty have had little or no exposure to instructional design and assessment and are not prepared to jump into learner-centered programs that routinely assess student learning. Increasing numbers of campus leaders recognize the need for ongoing faculty development that begins with a new faculty orientation and that extends throughout faculty careers. These programs encourage faculty to reflect on their objectives, design effective learning environments, contribute to cohesive curricula, and examine their impact on students.

Faculty development support can be provided in many ways. Some institutions have well-funded faculty development offices, staffed by multiple, full-time personnel with specialized training. Others offer release time to a faculty member who accepts responsibility for learning more about instructional design and assessment and sharing what has been learned with peers. Some campuses appoint a committee and charge it with these responsibilities. Grassroots faculty development programs are common, and they may involve brown-bag lunchtime discussions of personal experiences, reflections on teaching and learning, or selected readings. The faculty development literature is large and growing, supported by faculty who conduct scholarship of teaching studies and other professionals who examine pedagogical issues in higher education. Instructors who work without faculty development support face enormous challenges if they are to move into learner-centered instructional modes and assessment on their own.

Lopez (1999) reviewed almost 1,000 colleges and universities that are accredited by the North Central Association of Colleges and Schools to identify reasons why progress on assessment was prevented or delayed. She isolated eight major reasons:

1) Problems in engaging faculty and students in assessment.

2) Failure to develop explicit learning goals and objectives.

3) Failure to identify appropriate assessment techniques.

4) Problems with data collection or data interpretation.

5) Failure to review assessment results and act on them.

6) Failure to provide funding to support assessment efforts.

7) Failure to integrate assessment results into campus-wide decision-making, such as budgeting.

8) Failure to establish appropriate collaboration among all campus professionals.

Many of these aspects are under faculty control, such as the development of learning objectives, but faculty generally require training and assistance to do this well. In addition, she concluded that an institution-wide commitment to educational effectiveness increases the likelihood that assessment programs will be successful. This requires leaders who understand the formative nature of assessment, fund assessment initiatives, integrate assessment into campus operations, and ensure that campus structures support and reward collaboration.

Lopez (1999) found that a strong assessment committee often plays a key role in the development of effective assessment programs. She concluded that these committees work best when members are respected by their colleagues. Effective committee members advocate for assessment, are well trained in assessment methodology, and are willing to provide individual consultation and program support. This may require considerable campus investment in assessment, but unfunded mandates often fail and campus professionals may need extensive support to initiate assessment programs.

Institutions vary greatly in their commitment to assessment. The National Center for Postsecondary Improvement supported a multiyear study to identify how institutions promote and use outcomes assessment (Peterson & Vaughan, 2002). Researchers examined the extent of assessment activity and the impact this activity had on campus functioning in over 1,300 colleges and universities. One of their major conclusions was that campuses that conduct assessment mainly to respond to external mandates (such as accreditation requirements) do less assessment and are less likely to use assessment results than campuses that conduct assessment for internal reasons. They concluded that effective assessment focuses on improvement rather than accountability. Like Lopez, Peterson and Vaughan concluded that institutions with more comprehensive internal support were the most likely to have effective assessment programs.

These researchers more thoroughly investigated institutions with strong assessment programs. They found that the three most effective campuses had institutionalized assessment: "assessment was not a separate activity or process but was closely integrated with a broader approach to academic management, teaching, and curriculum improvement efforts" (Peterson & Vaughan, 2002, p. 42). All three provide ongoing training and support for assessment. Faculty on one of these campuses have access to a well-respected "Unit for Curricular and Instructional Innovation" and routinely integrate assessment results into program review and improvement. On another, assessment is integrated into ongoing strategic planning, and faculty regularly combine assessment results from their own studies with results from the campus-wide institutional research office. The third campus has an institutional focus on continuous improvement. Faculty and administrators integrate assessment results into strategic planning and use institution-wide quality indicators as well as program-specific quality indicators.

Peterson and Vaughan (2002) concluded that effective assessment requires four types of leadership:

- "Externally Oriented Leadership." A president or other leader advocates for institutional control of assessment with relevant funding agencies, governing bodies, and accrediting organizations and maintains positive relationships with these external groups.

- "Strategic Leadership." A chief academic officer or other administrator advocates for and integrates assessment into campus policies and procedures.

- "Process Leadership." A person or group provides training, consulting, and general support for effective assessment.

- "Technical Leadership." A person or group provides technical support in assessment methodology, data analysis, and data base management. (pp. 43-44)

All four are unlikely to be found in one person, and all were present on the campuses with the most effective assessment programs. As you review this list, consider who on your campus serves or could serve in these roles.

These findings present a challenge to faculty who are only beginning to integrate assessment into their activities or who want to improve the effectiveness of their assessment efforts. Effective assessment is most likely to develop in an institutional culture that values and supports assessment, and this culture requires active, continuing leadership of key administrators, faculty, and staff.

Some Friendly Suggestions

Most faculty and institutional leaders begin working on assessment in response to an external mandate, usually from an accrediting body. This mandate often convinces campus leaders to allocate resources and energy to this enterprise. The reason to do assessment, though, is to improve student learning. Professional educators owe it to their students to plan and implement a cohesive curriculum, and they should assess the impact of this curriculum on student learning and make adjustments when necessary.

Although the transition to becoming learner-centered can be time-consuming and sometimes painful, the end result should be a cohesive learning environment marked by clear expectations for the roles of faculty, administrators, staff, fieldwork supervisors, and students. Here are a few friendly suggestions to make the transition more pleasant and productive.

Don't skip steps. Remember the six steps defined in Chapter 1 (develop learning objectives, check for program alignment, develop an assessment plan, collect data, use results, and examine assessment processes)? It is tempting to start with some readily available, off-the-shelf product, such as a published test, to frame assessment efforts. The likely result is an assessment effort that ends up with people shrugging their shoulders and ignoring results. Spend the time to identify your learning objectives, align activities, and design an assessment plan.

Keep it simple. Keep your assessment plan simple and focused, so it is meaningful, manageable, and sustainable. Faculty are intelligent, creative people who can easily devise complicated structures. They may be able to carry off an assessment or two using that structure, but a series of simple, well-conceived assessment studies that can be completed under realistic constraints are much more likely to result in the incremental improvements that mark sustainable assessment programs.

Never test the depth of the water with both feet. Think of each assessment study as a pilot study and examine the process to be sure that it has formative validity. If it doesn't work well, refine it or find a better strategy.

Stay focused on the learner. Overcoming old habits is difficult, and faculty who move from teacher-centered models that cover content may require frequent reminders. We do assessment to improve student learning, and to do this well, we have to systematically focus on what our students actually learn.

Close the loop. Don't collect data for the sake of collecting data. Good assessment has impact. If you document deficiencies, act to remedy them.

Be professional. Treat colleagues and those who provide assessment data with respect. Assessment efforts that are professional are more likely to be sustainable and effective.

Get help. Locate faculty development or assessment professionals or colleagues who can help you. They may have experience using the assessment strategies you want to implement, and they may be able to help you address issues that arise.

Work together. Colleges and universities have an important mission, and this mission is best accomplished when campus professionals share a vision and coordinate their efforts to help realize it. Campus leaders have the responsibility to create and support an infrastructure that helps members in their institutions take pride in their accomplishments and face their challenges.

GLOSSARY

Absolute attainment assessment. Assessment determines how well students have mastered learning objectives. The emphasis is on absolute attainment, rather than value-added–do students exhibit mastery of learning objectives at acceptable levels?

Accreditation. Certification that programs or institutions have appropriate infrastructure, policies, and services to support their operations and that they are accomplishing their mission.

Alignment matrix. A matrix (table) that shows the relationship between two sets of categories, such as the relationship between program and course learning objectives.

Analytic rubric. A rubric for making a series of judgments, each assessing a characteristic of the product being evaluated.

Anonymity. Data elements cannot be associated with individual respondents.

Assessment. The collection and use of evidence to improve a product or process.

Assessment steps (for program assessment). Faculty develop learning objectives, check for alignment between the curriculum and the objectives, develop and implement an assessment plan, use results to improve the program, and routinely examine the assessment process and correct it, as needed.

Authentic assessment. The assessment process is similar to or embedded in relevant real-world activities.

Autonomy. Research participants have the right to self-determination and to make decisions about participation without undue pressure that would reduce this right.

Benchmark. A criterion for assessing results compared to an empirically developed standard.

Beneficence. The assessment study is designed to maximize possible benefits and to minimize or eliminate possible harm.

Bias. Systematic under- or over-estimates of what is being assessed.

Bloom's taxonomy. A popular scheme for defining depth of processing.

Calibration (norming). Evaluators are normed or calibrated so they consistently apply standards in the same way.

CHEA. The Council on Higher Education Accreditation (CHEA) certifies American accreditation agencies.

Checklist. A survey format that provides a list of options that can be selected.

Classroom assessment. Assessment to improve the teaching of specific courses and segments of courses.

Close the loop. Faculty discuss assessment results, reach conclusions about their meaning, determine implications for change, and implement them.

Closed-ended questions. Questions which require brief answers. Response options may be predetermined by the data collector.

Closing questions. Interview or focus group questions that bring closure to the process.

Coding scheme. A description of how to categorize responses in a content analysis.

Coefficient alpha. An internal consistency reliability estimate based on correlations among all items on a test.

Cohesive curriculum. A curriculum which systematically provides students opportunities to synthesize, practice, and develop increasingly complex ideas, skills, and values.

Collective portfolio. Collections of student work that are created by faculty for assessment purposes.

Competence. Ethical faculty understand the assessment methodologies they use.

Competence interview. Test which is orally administered.

Compound question. A question with two or more parts. Such questions might confuse respondents.

Confidentiality. The person who conducts the assessment study is aware of who participated, but does not disclose this information.

Consensus. A decision-making process in which a group seeks to maximize the input and support of all participants.

Construct validity. A form of validity based on testing predictions made using the theory or construct underlying the procedure.

Content analysis. Summarizing a set of communications by analyzing common themes and highlighting important issues.

Criterion-related validity. How well results predict a phenomenon of interest.

Data ownership. Who has control over the assessment data–who has the right to see the data or allow others to see them?

Data security. Access to assessment data is controlled.

Deception. Giving incorrect or misleading information to research participants.

Deep learning. Learning which makes knowledge personal and relevant to real-world applications.

Demographic characteristics. Individual characteristics such as age and sex.

Depth of processing. Degree of command of what is learned, ranging from knowledge of facts to the ability to use information to solve problems, create new ideas, and evaluate relative merit.

Developmental assessment. Repeated assessment information on individual students is used to track, verify, and support student development.

Developmental portfolio. A portfolio designed to show student progress by comparing products from early and late stages of the student's academic career.

Differences between ratings. An indicator of inter-rater reliability.

Direct measure. Students demonstrate that they have achieved a learning objective.

Disclosure of rights. Data collectors inform potential participants of their rights, such as their right not to participate and to know the degree of confidentiality associated with their responses.

Dual relationships. Participants in assessment projects have more than one relationship to the person collecting or analyzing the data, such as student-teacher or employee-employer relationships.

Educational effectiveness. How well a program or institution promotes student development.

Embedded assessment. Assessment activities occur in courses. Students generally are graded on this work, and some or all of it also is used to assess program learning objectives.

Exploitative relationships. Taking advantage of people over whom one has authority, such as students, supervisees, employees, and research participants.

Face validity. A form of validity determined by subjective evaluation by test takers or by experts in what is being assessed.

Fair and accurate reporting of results. Assessment reports are based on data, not on the assessor's desires, biases, or other factors extrinsic to the assessment process.

Focus groups. Planned discussions among groups of participants who are asked a series of carefully constructed questions about their beliefs, attitudes, and experiences.

Formative assessment. Assessment designed to give feedback to improve what is being assessed.

Formative validity. How well an assessment procedure provides information that is useful for improving what is being assessed.

Generalizable results. Results that accurately represent the population that was sampled.

Goals. General statements about knowledge, skills, attitudes, and values expected in graduates.

Halo effect. A problem that occurs when judgments are influenced by each other.

Harm. Physical or emotional/psychological damage to research participants.

High-stakes testing. Testing that has important implications for test takers, such as determining if individuals can be admitted into college.

Holistic rubric. A rubric that involves one global, holistic judgment.

Impact. Assessment results in appropriate changes to what is being assessed.

Indirect measure. Students (or others) report perceptions of how well students have achieved an objective.

Informed consent. Participants agree to participate in assessment projects based on knowing the purpose of the project, the expected use of the data, the rights to not participate and to discontinue participation, and if data will be anonymous or confidential.

Intentional teaching. Designing learning experiences to help students develop mastery of specific learning objectives.

Internal consistency reliability. A reliability estimate based on how highly parts of a test correlate with each other.

Inter-rater reliability. How well two or more raters agree when decisions are based on subjective judgments.

Interview protocol. A script and set of instructions for conducting interviews.

Issue questions. Interview or focus group questions that address the topics of primary interest.

Justice. Participants in research projects are selected fairly and without placing an undue burden on them.

Learning objective. A clear, concise statement that describes how students can demonstrate their mastery of a program goal.

Likert scale. A survey format that asks respondents to indicate their degree of agreement. Responses generally range from "strongly disagree" to "strongly agree."

Mission. A holistic vision of the values and philosophy of a program, department, or institution.

Negotiating an agreement. Principals agree in advance about the purposes of the project, the expected date of completion, ownership of the data, and who is to receive the report.

Norming. *See calibration.*

Norms/norm group. Results that are used to interpret the relative performance of others; for example, test results might be compared to norms based on samples of college freshmen or college graduates.

Objectivity. Faculty have an unbiased attitude throughout the assessment process, including gathering evidence, interpreting evidence, and reporting the results.

Open-ended question. A question which invites respondents to generate long replies, rather than just a word or two.

Opening questions. Questions in the warm-up phase of an interview or focus group.

Parallel forms reliability (or alternate forms reliability). A reliability estimate based on correlating scores collected using two versions of the procedure.

Partially closed-ended question. A question that provides an "other" option in addition to specified options. Respondents are invited to describe the "other" category.

Percentage of agreement. An indicator of inter-rater reliability.

Performance measure. Students exhibit how well they have achieved an objective by doing it, such as a piano recital.

Pilot study. An abbreviated study to test procedures before the full study is implemented.

Placement test. A test designed to identify where students should begin in course sequences, such as sequences in mathematics, composition, or foreign languages.

Portfolio. Compilation of student work. Students often are required to reflect on their achievement of learning objectives and how the presented evidence supports their conclusions.

Power test. A test which measures deep processing.

Primary trait analysis. The process of determining the primary traits (criteria) that faculty use to evaluate products.

Privacy. Research participants' right to determine what personal information they will disclose.

Program assessment. An ongoing process designed to monitor and improve student learning. Faculty develop explicit statements of what students should learn, verify that the program is designed to foster this learning, collect empirical data that indicate student attainment, and use these data to improve student learning.

Protocol. See interview protocol.

Purposeful sample. A sample created using predetermined criteria, such as proportional representation of students at each class level.

Qualitative assessment. Assessment findings are verbal descriptions of what was discovered, rather than numerical scores.

Quantitative assessment. Assessment findings are summarized with a number that indicates the extent of learning.

Recall item. A test item that requires students to generate the answer on their own, rather than to identify the answer in a provided list.

Recognition item. A test item that requires students to identify the answer in a provided list.

Reflective essays. Respondents are asked to write essays on personal perspectives and experiences.

Reliability. The degree of measurement precision and stability for a test or assessment procedure.

Representative sample. An unbiased sample that adequately represents the population from which the sample is drawn.

Response rate. The proportion of contacted individuals who respond to a request.

Rubric. An explicit scheme for classifying products or behaviors into categories that are steps along a continuum.

Sampling validity. How well a procedure's components, such as test items, reflect the full range of what is being assessed.

Showcase portfolio. A portfolio that documents the extent of learning by featuring the student's best work.

Specimen set. Test questions, instructions, score reports, and other materials that are provided to help professionals decide if the test is appropriate for their intended use.

Speed test. A test that measures how quickly students can do simple things.

Split-half reliability. An internal consistency reliability estimate based on correlating two scores, each calculated on half of the test.

Standardized test. A test which is administered to all test takers under identical conditions.

Structured group interview. A type of focus group with less interaction than traditional focus groups. Facilitation of such groups requires fewer skills than for traditional focus groups.

Structured interview. Interviewers ask the same questions of each person being interviewed.

Summative assessment. Assessment is designed to provide an evaluative summary.

Summative validity. Assessment accurately evaluates what is being assessed.

Surface learning. Learning based on memorization of facts without deep understanding of what is learned.

Survey. A questionnaire that collects information about beliefs, experiences, or attitudes.

Systematic sample. A sample collected using a systematic process, such as collecting products from every tenth student on a class list.

Test-retest reliability. A reliability estimate based on assessing a group of people twice and correlating the two scores.

Traditional focus group. Free-flowing discussions among participants, guided by a skilled facilitator who subtly directs the discussion in accordance with predetermined objectives.

Traditional measure. Students exhibit how well they have achieved an objective by taking traditional tests, such as multiple-choice tests.

Triangulation. Multiple lines of evidence lead to the same conclusion.

Unstructured interview. Interviewers are allowed to vary their questions across interviewees.

Validity. How well a procedure assesses what it is supposed to be assessing.

Value-added assessment. Student learning is demonstrated by determining how much students have gained through participation in the program.

Warm-up phase. The first segment of an interview or focus group.

Webfolio. A portfolio that is submitted on a web site or compact disc.

REFERENCES

Allen, M. J. (1995). *Introduction to psychological research.* Itasca, IL: Peacock.

Allen, M. J., Moe, M., & Roberts, S. (2000). *Assessment of three GE science objectives.* Retrieved August 27, 2002, from http://www.csub.edu/assessmentcenter/ScienceGEReport_6_00.htm

Allen, M. J., Noel, R., Deegan, J., Halpern, D., & Crawford, C. (2000). *Goals and objectives for the undergraduate psychology major: Recommendations from a meeting of California State University psychology faculty.* Retrieved November 17, 2002, from http://www.lemoyne.edu/OTRP/teachingresources.html#outcomes

Allen, M. J., & Yen, W. M. (2002). *Introduction to measurement theory.* Prospect Heights, IL: Waveland.

American Association for Higher Education. (1996). *9 principles of good practice for assessing student learning.* Retrieved November 14, 2002, from www.aahe.org/principl.htm

American Association for Higher Education. (2002). *Assessment forum: Frequently asked questions.* Retrieved August 7, 2002, from http://www.aahe.org/assessment/assess_faq.htm

American Association for Higher Education, American College Personnel Association, & National Association of Student Personnel Administrators. (1998, June). *Powerful partnerships: A shared responsibility for learning.* Retrieved May 31, 2002, from http://www.aahe.org/assessment/joint.htm

American College Personnel Association. (1996). *The student learning imperative: Implications for student affairs.* Retrieved September 17, 2002, from http://www.acpa.nche.edu/sli/sli.htm

American Educational Research Association. (1992). *Ethical standards of AERA.* Retrieved November 17, 2002, from http://www.aera.net/about/policy/ethics.htm

American Psychological Association. (1992). Ethical principles of psychologists and code of conduct. *American Psychologist, 47*, 1597-1611. Retrieved November 21, 2002, from http://www.apa.org/ethics/code1992.html

Angelo, T. A. (1999, May). *Doing assessment as if learning matters most.* Retrieved August 7, 2002, from www.aahebulletin.com/public/archive/angelomay99.asp

Angelo, T. A., & Cross, K. P. (1993). *Classroom assessment techniques: A handbook for college teachers* (2nd ed.). San Francisco, CA: Jossey-Bass.

Association of American Colleges and Universities. (2002). *Greater expectations: A new vision for learning as a nation goes to college.* Retrieved October 1, 2002, from http://www.greaterexpectations.org/

Association for Institutional Research. (2001). *Code of ethics.* Retrieved November 17, 2002, from http://www.airweb.org/page.asp?page=140

Banta, T., & Hamilton, S. (2002). Using portfolios to coordinate teaching and assessment of student learning. In A. Doherty, T. Riordan, & J. Roth (Eds.), *Student learning: A central focus for institutions of higher education* (pp. 77-80). Milwaukee, WI: Alverno College Institute.

Barr, R. B., & Tagg, J. (1995, November/December). From teaching to learning: A new paradigm for undergraduate education. *Change, 27*(2), 13-25.

Bauer, K. W., & Hanson, G. R. (2001). *Assessment tips for student affairs professionals.* Retrieved August 12, 2002, from http://www.naspa.org/netresults/PrinterFriendly.cfm?ID=544

Baxter, P. J. (2002). Mission-based student learning outcomes: Learn and serve. In A. Doherty, T. Riordan, & J. Roth (Eds.), *Student learning: A central focus for institutions of higher education* (pp. 85-88). Milwaukee, WI: Alverno College Institute.

Baxter Magolda, M., & Terenzini, P. T. (2002). *Learning and teaching in the 21st century: Trends and implications for practice.* Retrieved August 14, 2002, from http://www.acpa.nche.edu/seniorscholars/trends/trends4.htm

Belchier, M. J. (2000). *The National Survey of Student Engagement: Results from Boise State freshmen and seniors.* Retrieved December 2, 2002, from http://www2.boisestate.edu/iassess/Reports/Report%202000-04.htm

Bennett, W. E. (1987). Small group instructional diagnosis: A dialogic approach to instructional improvement for tenured faculty. *Journal of Staff, Program, and Organizational Development, 5*(3), 100-104.

Biggs, J. (1999). *Teaching for quality learning at university.* Buckingham, England: Open University Press.

Bloom, B. S. (Ed.). (1956). *Taxonomy of educational objectives: The classification of educational goals. Handbook I: Cognitive domain.* White Plains, NY: Longman.

Boise State University. (2002). *Institutional assessment reports on-line.* Retrieved October 23, 2002, from http://www2.boisestate.edu/iassess/Reports /REPORTS.HTM

California State University, Sacramento, Department of Sociology. (2000). *Assessment of and reflections on the collective portfolio.* Retrieved September 18, 2000, from http://www.csus.edu/psa/soc_v1/1Acad_Data_portfolio.htm

California State University, San Bernardino. (2002). *Annual status reports by college and program.* Retrieved December 16, 2002, from http:// gradstudies.csusb.edu/outcome/statusrpt.html

Cerbin, W., & Beck, T. (2002). Collaboration to create department-based student learning outcomes. In A. Doherty, T. Riordan, & J. Roth (Eds.), *Student learning: A central focus for institutions of higher education* (pp. 129-132). Milwaukee, WI: Alverno College Institute.

Cessna, M. A. (2002). Faculty collaboration through reflective practice teaching circles. In A. Doherty, T. Riordan, & J. Roth (Eds.), *Student learning: A central focus for institutions of higher education* (pp. 73-76). Milwaukee, WI: Alverno College Institute.

Chapman, D. (2002). Using problem-based learning to engage students in the thinking and practice of disciplines. In A. Doherty, T. Riordan, & J. Roth (Eds.), Student learning: A central focus for institutions of higher education (pp. 105-108). Milwaukee, WI: Alverno College Institute.

Christiansen, D. (2002). Articulating learning outcomes and designing courses with the outcomes in mind. In A. Doherty, T. Riordan, & J. Roth (Eds.), *Student learning: A central focus for institutions of higher education* (pp. 117-120). Milwaukee, WI: Alverno College Institute.

College of William and Mary. (2002). *College of William and Mary's report of institutional effectiveness.* Retrieved August 21, 2002, from http://roie.schev. edu/four_year/CWM/body.asp?&c=1

Conference on College Composition and Communication. (1995). Writing assessment: A position statement. *College Composition and Communication, 46*(3). Retrieved August 7, 2002, from http://www.ncte.org/ccc/ 12/sub/state6.html

Council for Higher Education Accreditation. (1998). *CHEA recognition.* Retrieved August 10, 2002, from http://www.chea.org/About/ Recognition.cfm

Cunningham, P. (2002). Using individual student and program assessment data to improve learning. In A. Doherty, T. Riordan, & J. Roth (Eds.), *Student learning: A central focus for institutions of higher education* (pp. 97-100). Milwaukee, WI: Alverno College Institute.

Cuseo, J. B. (2002). *Assessment of the first-year experience: Six significant questions.* Retrieved August 6, 2002, from http://www.brevard.edu/fyc/listserv/remarks/cuseo600.htm

Davis, B. G. (1993). *Tools for teaching.* San Francisco, CA: Jossey-Bass.

Diamond, R. M. (1997). *Designing & assessing courses & curricula: A practical guide* (rev. ed.). San Francisco, CA: Jossey-Bass.

Doherty, A., Riordan, T., & Roth, J. (Eds.). (2002). *Student learning: A central focus for institutions of higher education.* Milwaukee, WI: Alverno College Institute.

Duch, B. J., Groh, S. E., & Allen, D. E. (Eds.). (2001). *The power of problem-based learning: A practical "how to" for teaching undergraduate courses in any discipline.* Sterling, VA: Stylus.

Eder, D. J. (2001). Accredited programs and authentic assessment. In C. A. Palomba & T. W. Banta (Eds.), *Assessing student competence in accredited disciplines: Pioneering approaches to assessment in higher education* (pp. 199-216). Sterling, VA: Stylus.Erwin, T. D. (1991). *Assessing student learning and development: A guide to the principles, goals, and methods of determining college outcomes.* San Francisco, CA: Jossey-Bass.

Facione, N. C., & Facione, P. A. (1996). *Student outcomes assessment: Opportunities and strategies.* Retrieved August 7, 2002, from http://www.calpress.com/outcome.html

Ferris State University. (2002). *General education assessment at Ferris State University.* Retrieved August 7, 2002, from http://www.ferris.edu/HTMLS/academics/gened/assess.htm

Gardner, J. (2000, September 1). *The jury is in.* Retrieved August 12, 2002, from http://www.brevard.edu/fyc/listserv/remarks/gardner900.htm

George Mason University. (2001). *2001 graduating senior survey results.* Retrieved October 21, 2002, from http://assessment.gmu.edu/results/gss/2001/index.cfm

Georgetown University, Medical Center. (2001). *Orientation focus group.* Retrieved October 22, 2002, from http://data.georgetown.edu/schmed/ead/gu/researchproj/reports/orientationfg.cfm

Gromko, M. H., & Hakel, M. D. (2002). Evolution of learning outcomes. In A. Doherty, T. Riordan, & J. Roth (Eds.), *Student learning: A central focus for institutions of higher education* (pp. 41-44). Milwaukee, WI: Alverno College Institute.

Gronlund, N. E. (1991). *How to write and use instructional objectives* (4th ed.). New York, NY: Macmillan.

Halpern, D. F., & Associates. (1994). *Changing college classrooms: New teaching and learning strategies for an increasingly complex world.* San Francisco, CA: Jossey-Bass.

Harris, M. J. (2002). Faculty collaboration to teach and assess for communication and higher level thinking. In A. Doherty, T. Riordan, & J. Roth (Eds.), *Student learning: A central focus for institutions of higher education* (pp. 33-36). Milwaukee, WI: Alverno College Institute.

Heffernan, K. (2001). *Fundamentals of service-learning course construction.* Providence, RI: Campus Compact.

Hilgers, T. L., Bayer, A. S., Stitt-Bergh, M., & Taniguchi, M. (1995, February). Doing more than "thinning out the herd": How eighty-two college seniors perceived their writing-intensive classes [Electronic version]. *Research in the Teaching of English, 29*(1), 59-87. Retrieved December 14, 2002, from http://www.mwp.hawaii.edu/doingmorethan.htm

Holst, S., & Elliott, G. (2002, May). *Finding the artificial intelligence and assessment—Best tool for the job.* Paper presented at the Pacific Planning, Assessment & Institutional Research Conference, Honolulu, HI.

Honan, J. P., & Rule, C. S. (2002). *Using cases in higher education: A guide for faculty and administrators.* San Francisco, CA: Jossey-Bass.

Honan, W. H. (2002, August 14). *The college lecture, long derided, may be fading.* The New York Times. Retrieved August 21, 2002, from http://www.nytimes.com

IDEA Center. (1998, Spring). *Kansas State University general education senior interviews: Faculty training.* Manhattan, KS: IDEA Center.

Impara, J. C., & Plake, B. S. (Eds.). (2001). *The fourteenth mental measurements yearbook.* Lincoln, NE: University of Nebraska Press.

Jessen, R., & Patton, J. (2002). *Portland State University & the College Classroom Environment Scale.* Retrieved August 22, 2002, from http://www.brevard.edu/fyc/listserv/remarks/jessenandpatton2.htm

Johnson, D. W., & Johnson, F. P. (1997). *Joining together: Group theory and group skills* (6th ed.). Needham Heights, MA: Allyn and Bacon.

Joint Committee on Testing Practices. (1994). *Code of fair testing practices in education*. Retrieved August 7, 2002, from http://ericae.net/code.htm

Klor De Alva, J., & Slobodzian, K. A. (2001). University of Phoenix: A focus on the customer. In C. A. Twigg (Ed.), *Innovations in online learning: Moving beyond no significant difference*. Retrieved August 28, 2002, from http://www.center.rpi.edu/PewSYm/Mono4cs.html

Kottke, J. L., & Schultz, K. S. (1997). Using an assessment center as a developmental tool for graduate students: A demonstration. *Journal of Social Behavior and Personality* [Special issue], *12*(5), 289-302.

Krumme, G. (2002). *Major categories in the taxonomy of educational objectives*. Retrieved September 5, 2002, from http://faculty.washington.edu/krumme/guides/bloom.html

Lee, V. S. (2002). Coordinating campus initiatives through a focus on student learning outcomes. In A. Doherty, T. Riordan, & J. Roth (Eds.), *Student learning: A central focus for institutions of higher education* (pp. 89-92). Milwaukee, WI: Alverno College Institute.

Light, R. (2001). *Making the most of college: College students speak their minds*. Cambridge, MA: Harvard University Press.

Loacker, G. (2002). Teaching students to develop the process of self assessment. In A. Doherty, T. Riordan, & J. Roth (Eds.), *Student learning: A central focus for institutions of higher education* (pp. 29-32). Milwaukee, WI: Alverno College Institute.

Lopez, C. (1998, March). *The commission's assessment initiative: A progress report*. Retrieved August 2, 2002, from www.ncahigherlearningcommission.org/AnnualMeeting/archive/index.html

Lopez, C. L. (1999). *A decade of assessing student learning: What we have learned; what's next?* Retrieved August 5, 2002, from www.ncahigherlearningcommission.org/AnnualMeeting/archive/index.html

Macpherson, A. (2001, January 8). *Grading and assessment*. Message posted to the POD listserv, archived at http://listserv.nd.edu/archives/pod.html

Madden, M. L., & Mulle, V. (2002). A gradual approach to articulating student learning outcomes. In A. Doherty, T. Riordan, & J. Roth (Eds.), *Student learning: A central focus for institutions of higher education* (pp. 121-124). Milwaukee, WI: Alverno College Institute.

Mager, R. F. (1997). *Preparing instructional objectives: A critical tool in the development of effective instruction*. Atlanta, GA: Center for Effective Performance.

Maki, P. (2002a, January 15). *Using multiple assessment methods to explore student learning and development inside and outside of the classroom.* Retrieved August 7, 2002, from http://www.naspa.org/NetResults/article.cfm?ID=558

Maki, P. (2002b, May). Moving from paperwork to pedagogy. *AAHE Bulletin.* Retrieved August 7, 2002, from www.aahebulletin.com/public/archive/paperwork.asp

Maki, P. L. (2002c). *Developing an assessment plan to learn about student learning.* Retrieved August 7, 2002, from http://www.aahe.org/assessment/assessmentplan.htm

Malaney, G. D. (1999). *Student affairs research, evaluation, and assessment: Structure and practice in an era of change.* San Francisco, CA: Jossey-Bass.

Mary Washington College. (2002). *Mary Washington College's report of institutional effectiveness.* Retrieved August 21, 2002, from http://roie.schev.edu/four_year/MWC/body.asp?c=1

McGury, S. (2002). Promoting consistency in the incorporation of outcomes into classroom teaching, learning, and assessment. In A. Doherty, T. Riordan, & J. Roth (Eds.), *Student learning: A central focus for institutions of higher education* (pp. 61-64). Milwaukee, WI: Alverno College Institute.

McKeachie, W. J. (1999). *Teaching tips: Strategies, research, and theory for college and university teachers* (10th ed.). New York, NY: Houghton Mifflin.

McMillin, J. D., & Noel, R. C. (2001). A focus group method for use in program assessment. In C. F. Hohm & W. S. Johnson (Eds.), *Assessing student learning in sociology* (2nd ed.) (pp. 122-137). Washington, DC: American Sociological Association.

Menges, R. J., Weimer, M., & Associates. (1995). *Teaching on solid ground: Using scholarship to improve practice.* San Francisco, CA: Jossey-Bass.

Middle States Commission on Higher Education. (1996). *Framework for outcomes assessment.* Retrieved August 7, 2002, from http://www.msache.org/msafram.pdf

Miller, W. R., & Miller, M. F. (1997). *Handbook for college teaching.* Sautee-Nacoochee, GA: Pinecrest.

Millis, B. (1999). *Using interactive focus groups for departmental course and program assessments.* Paper presented at the American Association for Higher Education Assessment Conference, Denver, CO.

Millis, B. J. (2001). *Using interactive focus groups for departmental course and program assessments.* Retrieved December 8, 2002, from http://www.brevard.edu/fyc/listserv/remarks/millis.htm

Morgan, D. L., & Krueger, R. A. (1998). *The focus group kit* (Vols. 1-6). Thousand Oaks, CA: Sage.

Moss, A., & Holder, C. (1988). *Improving student writing: A guidebook for faculty in all disciplines.* Dubuque, IA: Kendall/Hunt.

National Center for Postsecondary Improvement. (2002). *Phase two: National survey.* Retrieved August 10, 2002, from http://www.umich.edu/~ncpi/52/Survey.html

National Commission for the Protection of Human Subjects of Biomedical and Behavioral Research. (1979). *The Belmont report: Ethical principles and guidelines for the protection of human subjects of research.* Retrieved November 18, 2002, from http://ohsr.od.nih.gov/mpa/belmont.php3

National Council on Measurement in Education. (1995). *Code of professional responsibilities in educational measurement.* Retrieved November 18, 2002, from www.natd.org/Code_of_Professional_Responsibilities.html

National Institutes of Health. (2001, October 1). *The code of federal regulations, title 45, public welfare, part 46, protection of human subjects* (DHHS Publication No. 0-307-551). Washington, DC: U.S. Government Printing Office.

New Century College. (2002). *Integrative studies graduation portfolio.* Retrieved February 18, 2002, from http://www.ncc.gmu.edu/intsgradport.html

Nichols, J. O. (1995). *Assessment case studies: Common issues in implementation with various campus approaches to resolutions.* New York, NY: Agathon Press.

Nilson, L. B. (1998). *Teaching at its best: A research-based resource for college instructors.* Bolton, MA: Anker.

Noel, R. C. (2001a). *Assessment of two GE arts and humanities objectives.* Retrieved August 27, 2002, from http://www.csub.edu/assessmentcenter/Humanities6_01.htm

Noel, R. C. (2001b). *Program X focus group report.* Retrieved November 27, 2002, from http://www.csub.edu/assessmentcenter/samplereport.htm

Noel, R. C. (2002). *Information resources student computer lab and runner mail survey.* Retrieved October 22, 2002, from http://www.csub.edu/assessmentcenter/studentlabReportFinal.doc

Novak, G. M., Patterson, E. T., Gavrin, A. D., & Christian, W. (1999). *Just-in-time teaching: Blending active learning with web technology.* Upper Saddle River, NJ: Prentice Hall.

Office of Postsecondary Education. (2002). *Accreditation in the U.S.* Retrieved August 12, 2002, from http://www.ed.gov/offices/OPE/accreditation/accredus.html

Olivet College. (2002). *The Olivet plan portfolio program.* Retrieved August 19, 2002, from http://www.olivetcollege.edu/catalog/cat_op_portfolio.htm

Paine-Clemes, B. (2001, April 10). Don't be afraid to ask the students. *Exchanges: The Online Journal of Teaching and Learning in the CSU.* Retrieved October 22, 2002, from http://www.calstate.edu/ITL/exchanges/viewpoints/Dont_be_Afraid_pg1.html

Palomba, C. A., & Banta, T. W. (1999). *Assessment essentials: Planning, implementing, and improving assessment in higher education.* San Francisco, CA: Jossey-Bass.

Palomba, N. A., & Palomba, C. A. (2001). Assessment of student competence in business. In C. A. Palomba & T. W. Banta (Eds.), *Assessing student competence in accredited disciplines: Pioneering approaches to assessment in higher education* (pp. 121-139). Sterling, VA: Stylus.

Peterson, M. W., & Vaughan, D. S. (2002). Promoting academic improvement: Organizational and administrative dynamics that support student assessment. In T. W. Banta & Associates (Eds.), *Building a scholarship of assessment* (pp. 26-46). San Francisco, CA: Jossey-Bass.

Petrulis, R. (2002). Portfolio assessment of college-wide learning objectives. In A. Doherty, T. Riordan, & J. Roth (Eds.), *Student learning: A central focus for institutions of higher education* (pp. 93-96). Milwaukee, WI: Alverno College Institute.

Program Assessment Consultation Team. (2001). *ITV focus groups: Four perspectives on the ITV experience.* Retrieved October 23, 2002, from http://www.csub.edu/tlc/itvfocus.htm

Riggio, R. E., Aguirre, M., Mayes, B. T., Belloli, C. A., & Kubiak, C. R. (1997). The use of assessment center methods for student outcome assessment. *Journal of Social Behavior and Personality* [Special issue], *12*(5), 273-288.

Robbin, J., & Alvarez-Adem, M. (2001). *Quantitative Assessment Committee annual report, 2000-2001.* Retrieved August 7, 2002, from http://www.math.wisc.edu/~assess

Rogers, G. M., Williams, J., & Misovich, M. (2002). Institution-wide student learning outcomes: Developing an integrated system for institutional effectiveness. In A. Doherty, T. Riordan, & J. Roth (Eds.), *Student learning: A central focus for institutions of higher education* (pp. 101-104). Milwaukee, WI: Alverno College Institute.

183

Scarafiotti, C. (2001). Rio Salado College: A systems approach to online learning. In C. A. Twigg (Ed.), *Innovations in online learning: Moving beyond no significant difference.* Retrieved August 28, 2002, from http://www.center.rpi.edu/PewSYm/Mono4cs.html

Scholarship of Teaching & Learning at Indiana University Bloomington. (2002). *Books & journals relating to SOTL.* Retrieved November 21, 2002, from http://www.indiana.edu/~sotl/resources.html

Seybert, J. (2002). *An "institutional portfolio" approach to assessment of general education.* Retrieved November 21, 2002, from http://old.jccc.net/admin/instres/cogout.htm

Sterken, R. (1999). *Individual student tracking project: A partnership for excellence report.* Retrieved August 7, 2002, from http://www.palomar.edu/alp/Portfolio.htm

Symonette, H. (1999). *Savvy assessment and evaluation skills.* Retrieved August 19, 2002, from www.diversityweb.org/research_and_trends/research_evaluation_impact/campus_climate_evaluation_tools/savvy_assessment.cfm

Truman State University. (1997). *The assessment almanac 1997.* Retrieved December 9, 2002, from http://assessment.truman.edu/data-as.stm

Truman State University. (2002). *The assessment almanac 2002.* Retrieved October 22, 2002, from http://assessment.truman.edu/data-as.stm

University of Arizona. (2000). *Tier one faculty survey results.* Retrieved October 22, 2002, from http://info-center.ccit.arizona.edu/~uge/gened/survey/fullresponse.html

University of Colorado at Boulder, Department of Fine Arts. (2000, May 11). *Activity in 1999-2000.* Retrieved August 7, 2002, from http://www.colorado.edu/pba/outcomes/units/fine.htm

University of Colorado at Boulder, Department of Physics. (2001). *Department of physics.* Retrieved August 7, 2002, from http://www.colorado.edu/pba/outcomes/units/phys.htm

University of Illinois at Urbana-Champaign, Department of Electrical and Computer Engineering. (2000). *ECE Illinois ABET evaluation.* Retrieved October 21, 2002, from http://www.ece.uiuc.edu/abet/facsurvCE.html

University of Massachusetts. (2002). *Project Pulse.* Retrieved December 2, 2002, from http://www-saris.admin.umass.edu/saris/pp_home.html

University of North Carolina. (1998). *Benchmarking undergraduate satisfaction.* Retrieved October 21, 2002, from http://www2.acs.ncsu.edu/UPA/survey/reports/sophsr98/benchmark98.htm

University of Saskatchewan. (1999). *Student outcomes survey templates.* Retrieved February 27, 2003, from http://www.usask.ca/vpacademic/ spr/surveytemplates.html

University of Wisconsin Oshkosh, Department of English. (n.d.). *English department assessment program: Committee responsibilities.* Retrieved October 23, 2002, from http://www.english.uwosh.edu/assess/committee.html

Upcraft, M. L., & Schuh, J. H. (1996). *Assessment in student affairs: A guide for practitioners.* San Francisco, CA: Jossey-Bass.

U.S. Department of Education. (2002). *Protection of human subjects in research.* Retrieved February 27, 2003, from http://www.ed.gov/offices/OCFO/ humansub.html

Walvoord, B. E., & Anderson, V. J. (1998). *Effective grading: A tool for learning and assessment.* San Francisco, CA: Jossey-Bass.

Wehlburg, C. (1999, May). How to get the ball rolling: Beginning an assessment program on your campus. *AAHE Bulletin, 51*(9), 7-9.

Weimer, M. (2002). *Learner-centered teaching: Five key changes to practice.* San Francisco, CA: Jossey-Bass.

Wergin, J. F. (1999, February). Evaluating department achievements: Consequences for the work of faculty. *AAHE Bulletin.* Retrieved August 13, 2002, from www.aahebulletin.com/public/archive/dec99f1.asp

Wiggins, G. (1998). *Educative assessment: Designing assessments to inform and improve student performance.* San Francisco, CA: Jossey-Bass.

Winston, R. B., Vahala, M. E., Nichols, E. C., Gillis, M. E., Wintrow, M., & Rome, K. D. (1994). A measure of college classroom climate: The College Classroom Environment Scales. *Journal of College Student Development, 35*(1), 11-35.

Wright, B. D. (2002). Accreditation and the scholarship of assessment. In T. W. Banta & Associates (Eds.), *Building a scholarship of assessment* (pp. 240-258). San Francisco, CA: Jossey-Bass.

Zlatic, T. D. (2001). Redefining a profession: Assessment in pharmacy education. In C. A. Palomba & T. W. Banta (Eds.), *Assessing student competence in accredited disciplines: Pioneering approaches to assessment in higher education* (pp. 49-70). Sterling, VA: Stylus.

INDEX